NOAH'S ARK

Noah's Ark

(Kashti-e-Nuh)

Hazrat Mirza Ghulam Ahmad

The Promised Messiah & Mahdi
Founder of the Ahmadiyya Muslim Community

ISLAM INTERNATIONAL PUBLICATIONS LIMITED

Noah's Ark

Written by Hazrat Mirza Ghulam Ahmad
The Promised Messiah and Mahdi, peace be upon him,
Founder of the Ahmadiyya Muslim Community

First Published in Urdu in Qadian, India, in 1902
Present English translation published in the UK in 2016
Reprinted (with minor corrections) in UK in 2018

Published by:
Islam International Publications Ltd.
Unit 3, Bourne Mill Business Park,
Guildford Road, Farnham, Surrey UK, GU9 9PS

Printed in the UK at:
Raqeem Press
Farnham, UK

For more information please visit:
www.alislam.org

ISBN: 978-1-84880-072-4
10 9 8 7 6 5 4 3 2

Contents

Hazrat Mirza Ghulam Ahmad of Qadian
The Promised Messiah & Mahdi
(peace be upon him)

About the Author

Hazrat Mirza Ghulam Ahmad, peace be upon him, was born in 1835 in Qadian, India. From his early life, he dedicated himself to prayer, the study of the Holy Quran and other scriptures. He was deeply pained to observe the plight of Islam, which was being attacked from all directions. In order to defend Islam and present its teachings in their pristine purity, he wrote more than ninety books, thousands of letters and participated in many religious debates. He argued that Islam is a living faith, which can lead humanity to the achievement of moral and spiritual perfection by establishing communion with God.

Hazrat Mirza Ghulam Ahmad, peace be upon him, started experiencing divine dreams, visions and revelations at a young age. In 1889, under divine command, he started accepting initiation into the Ahmadiyya Muslim Community. He continued to receive divine revelations and was thereafter commanded by God to announce that he was the divinely appointed Reformer of the Latter Days, as prophesied by various religions under different titles. He claimed to be the same Promised Messiah and Mahdi whose advent had been prophesied by the Holy Prophet Muhammad, peace and blessings of Allah be upon him. The Ahmadiyya Muslim Community is now established in more than two hundred countries of the world.

After the demise of the Promised Messiah, peace be upon him, in 1908, the institution of *Khilafat* (successorship) was established to continue his mission, in fulfilment of the prophecies made in the Holy Quran and by the Holy Prophet Muhammad, peace and blessings of Allah be upon him. Hazrat Mirza Masroor Ahmad, may Allah be his Helper, is the Fifth Successor to the Promised Messiah, peace be upon him, and the present Head of the Ahmadiyya Muslim Community.

Publisher's Note

The words in the text in normal brackets ( ) and in between the long dashes—are the words of the Promised Messiah, peace be upon him, and if any explanatory words or phrases are added by the translator for the purpose of clarification, they are put in square brackets [ ].

References to the Holy Quran contain the name of the *Surah* [i.e. chapter] followed by a chapter:verse citation, e.g. *Surah Al-Jumu'ah,* 62:4, and counts *Bismillaahir-Rahmaanir-Raheem* [In the name of Allah the Gracious the Merciful] as the first verse in every chapter it appears.

The name of Muhammad[sa], the Holy Prophet of Islam, has been followed by the symbol [sa], which is an abbreviation for the salutation *Sallallaahu Alayhi Wa Sallam* (peace and blessings of Allah be upon him). The names of other Prophets and Messengers are followed by the symbol [as], an abbreviation for *Alayhis-Salaam* (peace be upon him). The actual salutations have not generally been set out in full, but they should nevertheless, be understood as being repeated in full in each case.

Publisher

Facsimile of the original Urdu title page printed in 1902

This revelation has been published in 'The Green Announcement'

This is revelation from God, which has been sent down to me in the form of Quranic verses.

اِصْنَعِ الْفُلْكَ بِاَعْيُنِنَا وَوَحْيِنَا اِنَّ الَّذِيْنَ يُبَايِعُوْنَكَ اِنَّمَا يُبَايِعُوْنَ اللّٰهَ يَدُ اللّٰهِ فَوْقَ اَيْدِيْهِمْ

Translation: Construct the ark before Our eyes and according to Our command. Those who swear allegiance to thee swear allegiance to God. The hand of God is over their hands.

The treatise 'Heavenly Inoculation' which has been prepared about the plague for my community.

It is named

Noah's Ark

The second name is

An Invitation to Faith

The third name is

Strengthening of Faith

اِرْكَبُوْا فِيْهَا بِسْمِ اللّٰهِ مَجْرٖىهَا وَمُرْسٰىهَا لَا عَاصِمَ الْيَوْمَ مِنْ اَمْرِ اللّٰهِ اِلَّا مَنْ رَّحِمَ

—*Part 12, Surah Hud*

Board this Noah's Ark. In the name of Allah is its course and its mooring. On this day, none can be saved from the decree of God, except by Him. It is only He who can show mercy.

5 October 1902

Published in Qadian by Hakeem Fazl Deen of Bhera at Ziya-ul-Islam Press for the guidance and teaching of my community and those who seek the truth.

Number of Copies Printed: 5,000

[Translation of the original Urdu title page]

Hasten towards this ark of ours, for it belongs to the All-Knowing Lord.

Translation: If you believe and if you are thankful – for God has Himself appointed the means for your deliverance – why should God punish you?

My heart bursts with grief for the people due to the plague; nay, this is no plague, it is a raging storm.

Part 5, An-Nisaa

The Treatise Noah's Ark

or

'Strengthening of Faith'

بِسْمِ اللهِ الرَّحْمٰنِ الرَّحِيْمِ [1]

نَحْمَدُهُ وَنُصَلِّى عَلٰى رَسُوْلِهِ الْكَرِيْمِ [2]

The Plague Vaccine

Part 10, Ruku 13 — [3] لَنْ يُّصِيْبَنَآ اِلَّا مَا كَتَبَ اللهُ لَنَا هُوَ مَوْلٰنَا وَ عَلَى اللهِ فَلْيَتَوَكَّلِ الْمُؤْمِنُوْنَ

Translation: *Surely, nothing shall befall us save that which God has decreed for us. He is our Lord and our Master. And only in Him should the believers put their trust.*

Gratitude is due to the eminent British government who, showing kindness to its subjects, has once again advised inoculation against the plague, and has undertaken the expenditure of hundreds of thousands of rupees for the welfare of the servants of God. In truth, it is the duty of wise subjects to welcome this undertaking with gratefulness. Anyone who views

---

[1] In the name of Allah the Gracious the Merciful. [Publisher]

[2] We praise Him and invoke His blessings upon His Noble Messenger. [Publisher]

[3] *At-Tawbah,* 9:51 [Publisher]

the inoculation with mistrust is immensely foolish and is his own enemy, for it has been observed time and again that this cautious government is averse to administering any harmful treatment, and prescribes only remedies that have been thoroughly tested and proven to be effective. It is against the norms of honesty and civility to attribute ulterior motives to a government which has, and continues to spend, hundreds and thousands of rupees and resources out of genuine sympathy for its subjects.

Unfortunate are the subjects who reach such a degree of mistrust. There can be no doubt that until now inoculation is by far the best physical remedy that the government has found, and there is no denying that this remedy has proven to be effective. It is the duty of all subjects to make use of the means that are available to them so that they may relieve the government of the pain it feels for them. This notwithstanding, we must say to this kind government with all due respect that had there not been a heavenly prohibition for us, we would have been the first among its subjects to **be inoculated.** The heavenly prohibition is that God in this age desires to show a heavenly **sign of His mercy** to mankind. Addressing me, He said: 'You and those who dwell within the four walls of your house; those who unconditionally follow you and are obedient to you, and who on account of true righteousness have become devoted to you, shall all be **safeguarded against the plague.** This will be a sign of God in the Latter Days so that He might demonstrate a distinction between people. But those who do not follow you completely are not of you. **Be not anxious** on their account.'

This is a divine directive, on account of which I, myself and all those who dwell within the four walls of my house have no need to be inoculated. For as I have mentioned, God—who is the Lord of heaven and earth, and beyond whose knowledge and power there is nothing—revealed to me long ago that He would save everyone who lives inside the four walls of this house from death by the plague, provided he gives up all antagonism and **enters into the allegiance of *Bai'at*[4]** in all sincerity, submission and humility. He must not be **arrogant**, wilful, proud, heedless or vain towards God's commands and His Appointed One, and his conduct ought to be in conformity with my teachings. He has also told me that Qadian will be saved from such ravages of the plague that cause people to die like dogs and become mad with grief and confusion, and that generally the members of this community, however large in number, will be safe against the plague as compared to my opponents. However, such of my followers may fall prey to the plague who do not fully abide by their pledge, or concerning whom there is some hidden reason in the knowledge of God. But in the end people will marvel and acknowledge that, by relative comparison, the support of God is

---

[4] Oath of allegiance to a religious leader. [Publisher]

with these people, and that He has saved them through His special mercy in a way that has no precedence.

Certain uninformed people will be startled to hear this, others will laugh, while others will denounce me as mad, and still others will wonder if such a God really exists who can send down His mercy without resorting to physical means. The answer is, yes, such a powerful God does indeed exist, and if He was not so, those who are close to Him would have died a living death. He is wonderfully Omnipotent and marvellous are His holy powers. While, on the one hand, He allows ignorant opponents to attack His friends like dogs, on the other hand He commands the angels to serve them. In the same way, when His wrath comes upon the world and His anger surges against the wrongdoers, God watches over and protects His chosen ones. Were it not so, the entire mission of the people of God would **end in disarray** and no one would be able to recognise them. His powers are infinite, but they are revealed to people in proportion to their belief. Those who are blessed with certainty and love, and sever all ties for Him, and have broken free from selfish habits, it is for their sake that miracles are shown. God does what He wills, but He chooses to demonstrate His miraculous powers only to those who break from their ill habits for His sake. In this day and age there are very few people who know Him and believe in His extraordinary powers. On the contrary, there are many who have no belief whatsoever in this All-Powerful God, whose voice is heard by everything and for whom nothing is impossible.

At this instance, let it be remembered that to seek treatment for the plague or other diseases is not a sin. In fact, it is recorded in a Hadith that there is no disease for which God has not created a remedy. However, I consider it a sin to throw doubt on this sign by recourse to inoculation, for it is a sign which God, for our sake, wishes to demonstrate clearly in the world. I dare not demean His true sign and His true promise by resorting to inoculation. If I did, I would be accountable for the sin of not believing in the promise that God has given to me. If I were to benefit from inoculation, then I should be grateful to the doctor who invented the vaccine, and not to God who promised me that He would protect everyone dwelling in this house.

I proclaim by way of insight that the promises of the Omnipotent God are indeed true. And I see the coming days as if they have already come. I am also convinced that the principal aim of this eminent government is to protect the people from the plague by any means. In order to be safeguarded from the plague, if the government were to discover a remedy more effective than the vaccine, it would happily adopt it. Clearly, therefore, the path that God has commanded me to follow does not conflict with the objectives of this eminent government.

Twenty years ago, a prophecy regarding this great affliction of the plague was recorded in my book *Barahin-e-Ahmadiyya* and it was also promised therein that my community would be greatly blessed. See *Barahin-e-Ahmadiyya* pages 518 and 519.

In addition to this, God Almighty has emphatically declared that He will deliver from the affliction of the plague those sincere inhabitants of my home who are not arrogant before Him and His Appointed One. In relative comparison to others, God will grant this community a special favour. It is possible that there may be the odd case in my community due to a weakness of faith or a lack of action or death at its appointed time or on account of other causes which are known to God. However, rare instances as these cannot constitute the general rule. Whenever a comparison is made, the majority is given precedence. The government has itself found after investigation that those who make use of the plague vaccine have a lower fatality rate than those who do not. Therefore, just as the occasional death does not diminish the value of the vaccination, similarly, if there are occasional instances of the plague in Qadian or a few members of this community die from the disease, the grandeur of this sign will not diminish. This prophecy has been recorded in accordance with the undefiled Word of God. It does not befit an intelligent person to mock heavenly decree impetuously, for it is the Word of God and not the utterances of a soothsayer; it comes forth from a vista of light, not from the darkness of conjecture.

These are the words of He who has raised the plague and who has the power to eradicate it. Our government will invariably give credence to this prophecy once it witnesses the wonder that the people of our community will remain **safe and sound** from the plague in much greater numbers than the vaccinated. I say with true conviction that if this prophecy is not fulfilled exactly as it has been publicised for over the last twenty to twenty-two years, then I am not from God. As a **sign** that **I am from Allah,** the sincere people who live in the four walls of my home shall be protected from death by this disease. And, in comparison to others, my entire community will be saved from the onslaught of the plague. The security enjoyed by my community will not be shared by other people. Qadian will be saved from such an outbreak of the plague, which causes utter destruction except in the rarest of circumstances. **Alas!** If only the people possessed pure hearts and feared God, they would be saved completely. For calamities are not sent upon anyone in the world because of theological differences. Such matters will be decided in the hereafter. In reality, the world is afflicted by chastisement because of the spread of evil, pride and rampant sin. Let it also be borne in mind that both the Holy Quran and even certain books of the

Torah[5] foretell that plague will break out in the time of the Promised Messiah. In fact, the Messiah, peace be upon him, also spoke of this in the Gospel. It is impossible for the prophecies of the Messengers to be revoked.

It should also be kept in mind that on account of this divine promise, it is necessary for me to eschew any human contingencies, lest our enemies attribute this divine sign to other agencies. However, in addition to this, should God Almighty Himself disclose any other means or remedy to me through His word, then such means or remedy would not contravene this sign, for they emanate from God who has manifested this sign. No one should labour under the illusion that if a rare death occurs on account of the plague within my community, this would vitiate the greatness and stature of this sign. In old times, **Moses** and Joshua, and ultimately our **Prophet,** peace and blessings of Allah be upon him, were commanded to slay with the sword those who first raised the sword against them and who shed the blood of hundreds. Furthermore, this was a sign from the Prophets, after which a grand victory was achieved. Yet, despite this, in the field of battle the truthful too were slain by the swords of the wrongdoers, but very few. Such a loss was not significant enough

---

[5] The occurrence of the plague in the time of the Promised Messiah is recorded in the following books of the Bible: *Zachariah* 14:12, *the Gospel of Matthew* 24:8 and *Revelation* 22:8*.

* In the King James Version, this reference is *Revelation* 22:18. [Publisher]

to spoil the grandeur of this sign. Accordingly, if on the rare occasion, some members from among my community were to contract the plague, owing to the reasons already specified, their affliction shall in no way diminish this divine sign. Is it not a magnificent sign that I repeatedly declare that God Almighty will manifest this prophecy as to leave no one who seeks the truth in any doubt concerning it; and that every such person will surely recognise that God has miraculously protected this community?

Indeed, as a result of this divine sign, the plague will cause this community to grow manifold and enjoy a level of success so unprecedented that it will be heralded with great astonishment. If God does not manifest some distinction between this community and others according to the prophecy, then the opponents, who have hitherto suffered one defeat after another, as I have written in my book *Nuzul-ul-Masih*, will be justified in proclaiming me a liar. Thus far, they have only managed to heap a curse upon themselves by rejecting me. For example, they raised an ongoing hue and cry that Atham[6] had not died within the fifteen month period, even though the prophecy was clearly worded that if he returned to the truth then he will not perish within the fifteen months. And it so happened that during the

---

[6] Abdullah Atham was a retired civil servant and a prominent Christian polemicist who famously debated with the Promised Messiah[as] on the truth of Christianity and Islam. The debate lasted from 22 May to 5 June 1893. [Publisher]

very course of our debate, he recanted from referring to the Holy Prophet, peace and blessings of Allah be upon him, as the antichrist before seventy respectable men. Not only this, but in the subsequent fifteen months, his silence and fear testified to his contrition. The grounds to this prophecy was that he had referred to the Holy Prophet, peace and blessings of Allah be upon him, as the antichrist and so his repentance benefited him only to the extent that he did not die within fifteen months, but he did ultimately perish. This was because the prophecy stated that whosoever out of the two of us was false in his beliefs would be the first to die. Therefore, he passed away before me. Similarly, other matters of the unseen that God has revealed to me which have come to pass at their appropriate time, number no less than ten thousand. By way of example, I have recorded only a hundred and fifty such signs in my book *Nuzul-ul-Masih*, which is to be published and I have complemented this with supporting evidence and witnesses. All of my prophecies have been fulfilled, or in the case of those prophecies which consist of two parts, at least one part has come true so far. Even if a person were to strive all his life in the hope of finding a prophecy that was uttered from my mouth, about which one could assert that it has remained unfulfilled, he will not be able to find a single one. However, out of shamelessness or ignorance, one is free to say whatever he likes. I emphatically declare that thousands of my prophecies, which are clear in nature, have been categorically fulfilled and hundreds of thousands of people are witness to this. With the exception of the Holy Prophet, peace and blessings of Allah be upon him, no similar example can be found from the Prophets of the past. If only my enemies had judged me by this criterion, their eyes would have been opened long ago. If they were able to present the like of these prophecies, I would be more than willing to give them a handsome reward.

I can only attribute mischievous and ignorant attempts to disprove my prophecies to wretchedness and ill-thinking. They would surely have to retract their assertions if asked to discuss the matter in a gathering that was held to ascertain the truth; or else they would have to be called shameless. The fulfilment of thousands of prophecies to the letter along with thousands of witnesses to attest to their truth, who are still alive, is not an insignificant matter. This is akin to showing God, the Lord of Honour and Glory. Has anyone ever witnessed a time, except for the era of the Prophet [Muhammad[sa]], when thousands of prophecies were made and the brilliant fulfilment of each and every one of them was testified to by thousands of witnesses? I am quite certain that the manner in which God Almighty now draws near and manifests Himself and reveals hundreds of matters of the unseen to His servant, is almost unprecedented in past ages. In this age, people will soon witness a manifestation of the **countenance** of God Almighty, as if He has descended from heaven. He kept Himself hidden for a very long time. He was rejected and remained silent, but now He shall conceal Himself no longer and the world will witness manifestations of His power the likes of which their forefathers never saw. This will come to pass because the earth has been corrupted and people have lost faith in the Creator of the heavens and the earth. They pay lip service to Him but their hearts are estranged from Him. That is why God has declared that now He will create a new heaven and a new earth. This means that the earth has perished, that is, the hearts of the people of earth have so hardened as if they are dead. The face of God has become hidden from them and heavenly signs of the past were all reduced to myth and legend. Thus, God has decreed to create a new heaven and a new earth.

What is this new heaven? And what is this new earth? A new earth means those pure hearts that God is preparing with His own hand, **which will be manifested by Him and through whom God will be manifested.** A new heaven means those signs which are being shown by His command at the hand of His servant. It is a pity, however, that the world has opposed this new manifestation of God. They have nothing in hand but tales; their God is spawned by their own fancies. Their hearts are crooked, their resolve is weary and their eyes are veiled. Other nations have lost the true God themselves, let alone those who have deified the offspring of men.

Look at the state of the Muslims; how far detached from God they are. They are bitter opponents of the truth, and are like sworn enemies of the path of righteousness. For example, there is the *Nadwat-ul-Ulama*, who claim to represent Islam, or the *Anjuman-i-Himayat-i-Islam Lahore*, who take the wealth of Muslims in the name of Islam. **Are these people well-wishers of Islam?** Are they **supporters** of the right path? Are they aware of the tribulations that have smothered Islam and are they cognizant of the methods of revival employed by God? I truthfully declare that if I had not come, their claims to support Islam might have been acceptable to some extent. But now these people **stand accused by God Himself**; for **despite claiming** to be supportive, they were the first to deny the star **of heaven** when it emerged.

Now what answer will they give to God who has sent me precisely at the appointed time? Alas, they are completely heedless. **The sun** has almost reached its zenith, but by their reckoning it is still **night**. God's **fountain gushes forth** but they continue to lament in their wastelands. A river of His **heavenly knowledge** flows before them but they are completely oblivious to it. His signs continue to become manifest but they remain utterly unmindful of them. In fact, not only are they unmindful but they harbour **hostility towards the community of God.** So these are their efforts for the sake of assisting, propagating and teaching Islam! However, will the **rejection** of these people **halt** the true will of God, which all the Prophets have testified to since the remotest

ages? Certainly not! Instead, God's prophecy, كَتَبَ اللهُ لَاَغْلِبَنَّ اَنَا وَرُسُلِى [7]
will **soon** be fulfilled. Ten years ago today, God testified in favour
of His servant by causing the sun and the moon to eclipse in
Ramadan. He caused the **luminary of day** and the **luminary of
night** to bear testimony in my favour and thus manifested **two
signs.** Similarly, in fulfilment of the prophecies of the Prophets,
He also showed two earthly signs:

(1) You read the first of these in the Holy Quran as stated:

وَ اِذَا الْعِشَارُ عُطِّلَتْ [8]

Then, in the Hadith as you read:

وَلَيُتْرَكَنَّ الْقِلَاصُ فَلَا يُسْعٰى عَلَيْهَا [9]

For the fulfilment of this a railway in the land of Hejaz i.e.
between Mecca and Medina is being constructed.

(2) The second sign is the plague, as God Almighty says:

وَ اِنْ مِّنْ قَرْيَةٍ اِلَّا نَحْنُ مُهْلِكُوْهَا قَبْلَ يَوْمِ الْقِيٰمَةِ اَوْ مُعَذِّبُوْهَا [10]

---

[7] Allah has decreed: 'Most surely I will prevail, I and My Messengers.'
(*Surah Al-Mujaadalah*, 58:22) [Publisher]

[8] And when the she-camels, ten-month pregnant, are abandoned. (*Surah At-
Takweer*, 81:5) [Publisher]

[9] The she-camels shall be abandoned and shall not be used. [Publisher]

[10] There is not a township but We shall destroy it before the Day of
Resurrection, or punish it... (*Surah Bani Israa'eel*, 17:59) [Publisher]

So, God introduced the railway in the land and also sent the plague so that the heaven and earth may bear witness. So **do not war** with God, as to war with Him will be sheer folly. In the past, when God decreed to make Adam a *Khalifah,* the angels put forth their plea. But was God held back by their submission? Now when He has raised the **second Adam,** He has declared: أَرَدْتُ أَنْ أَسْتَخْلِفَ فَخَلَقْتُ آدَمَ, that is, I decreed to raise a *Khalifah* and have thus decided to raise this Adam. Can anyone halt the will of God? So why do you present this worthless conjecture and not tread the path of certainty? Do not put yourself to trial and know for certain that there is no one who can frustrate the will of God. Such disputes are against the path of righteousness. But, should anyone be prey to doubt, there is another method. On the basis of God's revelation, I have received glad tiding that the group of individuals who pay heed to my words will be saved from the punishment of the plague and this has been published. Similarly, other people who possess heartfelt concern for the welfare of their people should also secure the good news from God Almighty that their co-religionists will be protected from the plague. Then, they too ought to publish this prophecy so that the public knows that they enjoy God's support. In fact, this too is a wonderful opportunity for the Christians who ever proclaim that salvation lies with the Messiah. Surely, in these days of peril, they too are obliged to deliver their fellow Christians from the plague. So, of **all these denominations,** the one whom God heeds the most will have to be considered as **accepted** by Him. Now, God has given everyone the opportunity to cease unnecessary indulgence in debates on earth and instead show the level of their acceptance so that they can be saved from the plague and their own truth may become evident as well. This is particularly true for the **Christian clergy** who have declared the Messiah **son of Mary** to be the saviour of the world and the hereafter. If they truly believe the Son of Mary to be the Lord of this world and the next, then they are **entitled** to witness a manifestation of **salvation** through his **atonement.** This will also ease the problems of the eminent government. In order to save their people and deliver them from the plague, the various denominations present in British India, who consider themselves true in their faith, ought to repair to their God whom they believe in, or any other being whom they deem worthy of worship besides God, and call on Him to save these afflicted souls. And they ought to attain a firm promise from their God and publish it in the form of announcements just as I have published this announcement. Not only is such a course wholly in the interest of all creation, but will also help establish the truth of their particular faith and shall also provide assistance to the government. What more does the administration desire than the deliverance of its people from the plague, by any means possible?

Finally, through the publication of this announcement, I wish to make it known to the members of my community—who are spread throughout the Punjab and elsewhere in India—that they are not prohibited from taking the vaccine. Should the government categorically order their vaccination, they ought to duly comply with this directive and have the vaccine administered to them. And it would be appropriate for those who are given a choice in this respect to avail it, if they do not fully follow the teachings that have been delivered to them; so that they do not stumble, or permit their own miserable state to spawn doubt regarding the promise of God in the minds of others. Below, I briefly expound on the teaching—which, if followed precisely, can stave off the onslaught of the plague—for anyone who may have an interest to know.

Our Teaching

Let it be clear that to affirm the covenant of *Bai'at* with the tongue alone amounts to nothing unless it is practiced with full, heartfelt resolve. Thus, whosoever fully acts upon my teachings enters that house of mine, concerning which God Almighty has promised in His Word:

$$\text{اِنِّیْ اُحَافِظُ کُلَّ مَنْ فِی الدَّارِ}$$

That is, I shall protect everyone who is within the four walls of your home. This should not be taken to mean only such people who dwell in my house made of brick and mortar; rather, this also refers to all those who follow me completely and dwell in my spiritual home. To follow me, it is necessary for them to believe that they have an Omnipotent, Self-Sustaining God, who is the Creator of all things, and whose attributes are eternal, everlasting and unchangeable. He has no father and no son. He is above suffering, being crucified and killed. He is such that despite being far, He is near; and despite being near, He is far. Despite being One, His manifestations are diverse. For a person who brings about a change in himself, He becomes a new God for him and deals with him by means of a new manifestation. Thus, such a person experiences a change in God according to the change in himself. Yet no change takes place in God, for He is eternally unchangeable and possesses complete perfection, but when a person undergoes a transformation and begins to move towards virtue, God manifests Himself to such a person in a new way. At the time of every improved condition that manifests itself in a person, the manifestation of God Almighty's power also reveals itself to a greater extent. He manifests His might in an extraordinary way only when an extraordinary change takes place in a person. This is the root of all extraordinary happenings and miracles. The God so described is the fundamental bedrock of my community. Believe in Him and give precedence to Him over your own souls and comforts and over all your relationships; show sincerity and loyalty in His cause by exhibiting courage in your practice. Worldly people do not prefer Him over their means, and their kith and kin, but you ought to, so that you may be counted in heaven as belonging to His community.

It has been the practice of God since the remotest ages to manifest signs of His mercy, but you can partake of it only when nothing separates you from Him, His will becomes your will, His desire becomes your desire, and you remain prostrate at His threshold at all times and in all conditions—whether of success or failure—so that He may do whatever He wills. If you do so, then God, who has for so long kept His countenance hidden, will manifest Himself in you. Is there anyone from among you who will **implement this** and seek His pleasure, without being dissatisfied by His will and decree? So when you encounter misfortune, you should step forth even more eagerly, for this is the means of your success. Exert all your power to spread the **Oneness** of God on earth. Show mercy to His servants and do not wrong them by your tongue or your hand or by any other means, and strive for the welfare of God's creation. Behave not arrogantly towards anyone even if he is your subordinate, and revile not anyone even if he should revile you. Become humble, tolerant, well-intentioned and compassionate towards God's creation so that you may be accepted by God.

There are many who show meekness, but they are wolves from within. There are many who outwardly appear clean, but from within they are serpents. You, therefore, cannot be accepted by

God unless you are the same inside and out. If you are above others, have mercy on the lowly and do not look down upon them. If you are learned, counsel the ignorant and do not degrade them with disdain. If you are wealthy, serve the poor, and do not treat them with arrogance and self-conceit.

Dread the ways of ruin and always be fearful of God. Adopt righteousness and worship not His creation. Cut asunder from everything to turn to your Master. Turn your hearts away from the world and become wholly His; live for Him alone and, for His sake, hate every impiety and sin, for He is Holy. Let every morning bear witness that you have spent the night in righteousness, and let every evening bear witness that you have spent the day with the fear of God. Be not afraid of the curses of the world, for they shall vanish before your eyes like smoke and cannot turn day into night. Fear instead the curse of God which descends from heaven and uproots its victims in both worlds. You cannot save yourselves with hypocrisy, for your God is He who sees the innermost depth of man. Can you then deceive Him? So become straightforward, clean, pure and truthful. If even a particle of darkness is left within you, it will dispel all your light. And if you possess even the slightest arrogance, hypocrisy, self-conceit or sloth, you are not worthy of being accepted. Be careful lest a few accomplishments delude you to think that you have sufficiently fulfilled your purpose. For God desires a complete transformation in your being and He demands from you a death whereafter He should revive you. Hasten to make peace with one another and forgive your brethren their sins. For he who is not inclined to make peace with his brother is wicked and will be cut off, because he is the cause of dissension. Part with your ego in every way and do away with mutual grievances. Be humble like the guilty, though truth be on your side, so that you may be forgiven. Do not feed your vanity, for those who are bloated cannot enter the gate to which you have been called.

How unfortunate is the one who does not believe in that which has come from the mouth of God and which I have set forth. If you desire that God should be pleased with you in heaven, unite with one another as though you were brothers from the same womb. The one who most forgives the transgressions of his brother is the more honourable among you. Unfortunate is the one who is obstinate and does not forgive. Such a person has no part in me. Be very fearful of God's curse, for He is Holy and Jealous. An evildoer cannot attain nearness to God. One who is arrogant cannot attain nearness to God. A wrongdoer cannot attain nearness to God. He who is unfaithful cannot attain nearness to God. Every such person who is not jealously protective for the sake of God's name cannot attain His nearness. Those who fall upon the world like dogs, ants and vultures, and find their comfort in the world, cannot attain nearness to God. Every impure eye is far from Him; every impure heart is unaware of Him. He who burns for His sake will be delivered from the fire; he who weeps for His sake will laugh; and he who cuts asunder from the world for His sake will find Him. Befriend God with a true heart, full sincerity and complete eagerness, so that He too may befriend you. Have mercy on your subordinates and your wives and your less fortunate brethren so that you too may be shown mercy in heaven. Become truly His, so that He too may become yours. The world is home to a thousand evils, one of which is also the plague. So hold fast to God with sincerity so that He should safeguard you against all calamities. No calamity visits the earth until there is a command from heaven, and no affliction is alleviated until mercy descends from heaven. So, you would be wise to take hold of the root rather than the branch. You are not prohibited from having recourse to the necessary means and appropriate remedies, but you are forbidden to rely upon them. Ultimately, the will of God will prevail. Complete trust in God, if one has the strength for it, is greater than all else.

An essential teaching for you is that you should not abandon the Holy Quran like a thing forsaken, for therein lies your life. Those who honour the Quran will be honoured in heaven. Those who give precedence to the Quran over every Hadith and every other saying will be given precedence in heaven. Today, there is no book on the face of the earth for mankind except for the Quran. The sons of Adam have no Messenger and Intercessor but **Muhammad, the Chosen One**, peace and blessings of Allah be upon him. Endeavour, therefore, to cultivate true love for this

22

Prophet of glory and majesty, and do not give precedence to anyone over him, so that in heaven you may be counted as those who have attained salvation.

Remember, salvation is not something that will be manifested after death. On the contrary, true salvation exhibits its light in this very world. Who is **the one who attains salvation**? Such a person is he who believes that God is true and that Muhammad, peace and blessings of Allah be upon him, is the **Intercessor** between God and all His creation, and that under the heaven there is no Messenger **equal in rank** to him, nor is there any book **equal in status** to the Quran. God did not desire that anyone should remain alive eternally, **but this Chosen Prophet lives forever**. To keep him alive forever, God has ordained that his spiritual and law-giving blessings would last until the day of resurrection. Finally, as a continuation of his spiritual blessings, God has sent unto the world the **Promised Messiah**—whose advent was essential for the **completion** of the edifice of Islam. It was necessary that the world should not come to an end until the dispensation of Muhammad had been granted a **spiritual** Messiah, as had been endowed to the Mosaic dispensation. This is indicated in the verse:

[11]

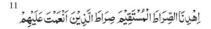

---

[11] Guide us in the right path—the path of those on whom Thou hast bestowed *Thy* blessings. (*Surah Al-Faatihah*, 1:6-7) [Publisher]

23

Moses was bestowed a treasure which earlier generations had lost, and Muhammad, peace and blessings of Allah be upon him, was bestowed the riches, which the dispensation of Moses lost. Now the dispensation of Muhammad has replaced the Mosaic dispensation, but it is thousands of times higher in status. The one sent in the likeness of Moses is greater than Moses and the one sent in the likeness of the Son of Mary is more exalted than the Son of Mary. Just as the Messiah son of Mary came in the fourteenth century after Moses, the Promised Messiah appeared in the fourteenth century after the Holy Prophet, may peace and blessings of Allah be upon him,[12] and he appeared at a time when the condition of the Muslims was similar to that of the Jews at the time of the advent of the Messiah son of Mary. **I am that Messiah.** God does what He wills. Foolish is the person who wars with Him and ignorant is the one who objects to his works and considers that they should have been otherwise. He has sent me with over ten thousand brilliant signs, one of which is the plague. So, in these calamitous times, my soul shall intercede only for such a person who sincerely enters my allegiance of *Bai'at* and wholeheartedly follows me and submerges themselves in obedience to me to the extent that they relinquish their own will.

O ye people who consider yourselves **members** of my

---

[12] The Jews unanimously believe in accordance with their history that Jesus appeared at the head of the fourteenth century after Moses. See Jewish history. (Author)

community! You will be **counted** as such in heaven when you truly tread upon the ways of **righteousness**. So, offer the five daily prayers in such fear and with such complete attention as though you were actually beholding God Almighty. Sincerely observe your fasts for the sake of God. Let everyone who is liable to pay the Zakat do so and anyone upon whom the Hajj has become obligatory and who face no hindrance ought to perform the pilgrimage. Do good in a handsome manner and discard vice with disgust. Bear well in mind that no action of yours, which is empty of righteousness, can reach God. **Righteousness** is the root of all goodness. No action that is rooted in righteousness will go in vain. It is inevitable that you should also be tried with various forms of anguish and misfortune, just as the faithful before you were tried. **Be on your guard,** lest you should falter. So long as you have a **firm relationship** with heaven, the earth can do you no harm. Whenever harm befalls you, it will be from your own hands and not from the hands of your enemy. Even if you lose all honour on earth, God will bestow eternal honour upon you in heaven. So do not forsake Him.

You will certainly suffer pain and many of your desires will not be fulfilled, but do not lose heart in such situations, for your God tries you to see whether you are steadfast in His path or not. If you desire that even the angels should praise you in heaven, then endure beating and remain joyful, hear abuse and be grateful, suffer setbacks but do not sever your relationship with God.

You are the last community of God, so practice virtue at its best. Anyone of you who becomes slothful will be cast out of the community like a foul thing and will die in regret and will be able to do no harm to God. **I** gladly **inform** you that your God truly exists. Though all are His creation, but He chooses the one who chooses Him. He comes to the one who goes to Him. He bestows honour upon him who honours Him.

Approach God with sincere hearts, and pure tongues, eyes and ears, for He will then accept you. What God requires of you, in the matter of belief, is that God is One and that Muhammad, peace and blessings of Allah be upon him, is His Prophet and *Khaatam-ul-Anbiyaa* [the Seal of the Prophets] and that he is the greatest of them all. After him there is no Prophet except one who is cloaked in the mantle of Muhammad[sa], by way of reflection. For a servant cannot be separated from his master, nor is a branch separable from its root. Thus, one who completely annihilates himself for his master is bestowed with the title of **Nabi** [Prophet] by God. Such a one does not break the seal of prophethood. When you look into a mirror, although there seems to be two, in reality there is only one. The distinction exists between that which is real and its reflection. Such is the will of God with respect to the Promised Messiah. This is also **the secret** behind the saying of the Holy Prophet, peace and blessings of Allah be upon him, when he stated: 'The Promised Messiah would be buried in my grave;' meaning, **he and I are the same** and completely identical.

Know for certain that **Jesus son of Mary** has died. His grave is in Mohalla Khanyar, Srinagar, Kashmir.[13] God Almighty Himself has spoken of his demise in His Beloved Book. For if the following verse [cited below] has some other implication, then where else has the death of Jesus son of Mary been mentioned in the Quran? If the verses regarding his death mean something else, as our opponents believe, then this would suggest that the Quran has nowhere addressed the issue of his death, and whether he would ever pass away. God has spoken of the death of our Prophet, but in the whole of the Quran, He has nowhere mentioned the death of Jesus. What is the secret behind this? If the verse فَلَمَّا تَوَفَّيْتَنِي كُنْتَ اَنْتَ الرَّقِيْبَ عَلَيْهِمْ [14] informs us of the death of Jesus, the clear implication of this verse is that he died before the

---

[13] **Note:** Christian researchers have also expressed this view. See *Supernatural Religion*, page 522.* For further information consult page 139 of my book *Tuhfa-e-Golarhviyyah*. (Author)

* In the revised edition of *Supernatural Religion* by Walter Richard Cassels, vol. 3 published in 1879 by Longmans, Green, and Co., this appears on pages 523-524. [Publisher]

[14] It is evident from this verse* that Jesus, peace be upon him, will not reappear in the world. For if he was to return to the world again, in such a case, it would be a mere lie for Jesus to respond by saying that he knew nothing of the decline of the Christians. Now as for such a person who returns to the world for a second time; lives for forty years; witnesses tens of millions of Christians deify him; breaks the cross and converts all of the Christians to Islam, how could he stand before his Lord on the Day of Resurrection and claim ignorance of the decline of the Christians? (Author)

*[*Surah Al-Maa'idah*, 5:118, Publisher]

Christians transgressed. And if the verse فَلَمَّا تَوَفَّيْتَنِى suggests that Jesus was lifted to heaven alive with his physical body, then why did God not mention in the Quran of the eventual death of a figure whose 'life' has led hundreds of thousands of people astray? It is as if God conferred on him eternal life, so that people may fall prey to idol-worship and lose their faith, and it would seem as if the people have not erred, but it is God who has done all this to lead them astray.

Remember, the religion of the cross cannot die unless the Messiah is allowed to pass away. After all, what benefit is there in considering him alive in contradiction to the teaching of the Quran? Let him die so that this faith [Islam] may live again. God manifested the death of the Messiah through His Word; and on the night of the *Mi'raaj*[1] the Messenger of Allah, peace and blessings of Allah be upon him, saw him dwelling among the dead. And yet you still do not believe in his death. **What manner of faith** is this? Do you prefer the tales of men over the Word of God? What kind of religion is this?[2] Not only did our Messenger, peace

---

[1] Spiritual ascension of the Holy Prophet[sa]. [Publisher]

[2] **Note:** There is a verse in the Holy Quran which clearly indicates that the Messiah and his mother travelled to Kashmir after the incident of the crucifixion. It says: وَاٰوَيْنٰهُمَآ اِلٰى رَبْوَةٍ ذَاتِ قَرَارٍ وَّمَعِيْنٍ 'We gave Jesus and his mother shelter on an elevated land which was a place of comfort and was provided with springs of clear water.' Here, God Almighty has depicted an illustration of Kashmir. According to the Arabic lexicon, the word *aawaa* is used to grant refuge against calamity or misfortune; and before the crucifixion, Jesus and his

and blessings of Allah be upon him, testify that he had seen Jesus among the souls of the dead, but even by his own death, the Prophet demonstrated that none of the Prophets who came before him were still alive. But, just as our opponents have abandoned the Quran, they have also renounced the Sunnah; for death is a part of the Sunnah of our Prophet. If Jesus was still alive then death would be a dishonour to our Messenger. For as long as you do not believe in the death of Jesus you will stand in defiance of both the Quran and Sunnah. I do not deny the greatness of Jesus, peace be upon him, despite the fact that I have been informed by God that the Messiah of Muhammad[sa] occupies a higher status than the Messiah of Moses. Nevertheless, I hold the Messiah son of Mary, in high esteem, inasmuch as I am spiritually the **Khaatam-ul-Khulafaa** [the Seal of the Caliphs] in Islam, just as the Messiah son of Mary was the *Khaatam-ul-Khulafaa* of the Israelite dispensation. The Son of Mary was the Promised Messiah of the Mosaic dispensation and I am the Promised Messiah of the dispensation of Muhammad[sa]; so I honour greatly the one whose name I bear. Anyone who asserts that I do not revere the Messiah son of Mary is mischievous and a liar.

---

mother underwent no period of hardship as would require refuge. It is thus established that it was only after the incident of the crucifixion that God Almighty led Jesus and his mother to this elevated land. (Author)

*[*Surah Al-Mu'minun*, 23:51, Publisher]

I honour not only the Messiah, but also his four brothers,[1] as all five of them were sons of the same mother. I also regard his two biological sisters as pious, for they are all from the womb of the Holy Virgin Mary. Mary's greatness lies in the fact that she abstained from marriage for quite a time and eventually yielded only due to the insistence of her elders during pregnancy. Certain people object that Mary married during her pregnancy, which is against the teachings of the Torah. In this way, she wrongfully broke her covenant of remaining a virgin and also opened the door to polygamy, since Mary agreed to enter into matrimony with Joseph the Carpenter, though he was already married at the time. However, I say that these were compelling circumstances, which happened to arise, and for this reason both ought to be looked upon with mercy rather than disdain.

I repeat that you should not be content with having made a superficial covenant of *Bai'at*, for this amounts to nothing. God looks at your hearts and will deal with you accordingly. Look here, I discharge the obligation of conveying my message by telling you that sin is a poison—do not consume it. Disobedience to God is a filthy death—safeguard yourselves against it.

---

[1] **Footnote:** Christ the Messiah had four brothers and two sisters who were related to Christ by blood and were the children of Joseph and Mary. The names of his four brothers are (1) Judas, (2) James, (3) Simon and (4) Justus. The names of his two sisters are (1) Assia and (2) Lydia. See *Apostolic Records* by Father John Allen Giles, London, 1886, pp. 159, 166. (Author)

Supplicate so that you might be granted strength. He who at the time of supplication does not believe that God has power over all things, except that which might be contrary to His promise, is not of my community. Whosoever does not give up lying and deceit, is not of my community. Whosoever is consumed by material greed and does not lift his eyes to look at the hereafter, is not of my community. Whosoever does not truly give precedence to religion over the world, is not of my community. Whosoever does not repent of every vice and every evil deed, such as drunkenness, gambling, lustful glances, deceit, bribery and every misappropriation, is not of my community. Whosoever does not observe the five daily prayers, is not of my community. Whosoever is not constant in supplication and does not remember God with humility, is not of my community. Whosoever does not discard the company of an evil one who influences him towards vice, is not of my community. Whosoever does not honour his parents and does not obey them in all matters that are not contrary to the Quran, and is careless in serving them diligently, is not of my community. Whosoever does not treat his wife and her relatives with gentleness and benevolence, is not of my community. He who refrains from doing even the least bit of good to his neighbour, is not of my community. He who does not desire to forgive an offender and harbours rancour, is not of my community. Every husband who deceives his wife, and every wife who deceives her husband, is not of my community. Whosoever breaks the covenant of *Bai'at* in any respect, is not of my community. He who does not truly believe in me as **the Promised Messiah and Awaited Mahdi,** is not of my community. Whosoever is unwilling to obey me in all that is good, is not of my community. Whosoever associates with my opponents and endorses what they say, is not of my community. Every adulterer, transgressor, drunkard, murderer, thief, gambler, deceiver, bribe-taker, usurper, tyrant, liar, forger and those who sit amongst them, and everyone who slanders his brothers or sisters and does not repent of his foul deeds, and does not abstain from evil company, is not of my community.

All these are poisons. You cannot consume this poison and survive; light and darkness cannot exist together. Everyone who possesses a crooked disposition and is not straightforward with God, can never achieve the blessing that is bestowed on the pure-hearted. How fortunate are those who cleanse their hearts and purify them of every impurity and swear an oath of loyalty to their God, for they will never be destroyed. It is not possible that God should humiliate them, for they are God's and God is theirs. They will be safeguarded at the time of every calamity. Foolish is the enemy who moves against them, for they are in the lap of God and enjoy His support.

Who is it that believes in God? Only those who are such as we have just described. Similarly, foolish is he who is inclined towards a fearless sinner, or one who is evil-minded and vicious, for he will destroy himself. Ever since God has created the heaven and earth, it has never happened that He should have ruined or destroyed or obliterated the righteous. On the contrary, he has always shown wonders in their favour and will also show them now. God is most Faithful and He manifests wondrous works for those who are loyal to him. The world desires to devour them and every enemy grinds their teeth at them, but He who is their friend, delivers them from every place of danger and bestows victory upon them in every field. How fortunate is the person who **never lets go the mantle** of God. We have believed in Him and we have recognised Him. **The God** of the whole world is He who has sent down His revelation to me, who has shown **mighty signs** in my support and who has sent me as the **Promised Messiah** in this age. There is no God beside Him, neither in heaven nor on earth. He who does not believe in Him is bereft of all good fortune and is ensnared in disgrace. The revelation I have received from God is as bright as the sun. I have seen that He alone is the Lord of the world and that there is none other than Him. Truly Omnipotent and All-Sustaining is the God whom we have found. How great are His powers of Him whom we have witnessed. The truth is that nothing is beyond Him except that which is contrary to His Book and His promise. So when you pray, do not be like ignorant naturalists who have in their own fancy devised a natural law which does not bear the seal of God's Book. They are the rejected and their prayers will not be accepted. They are blind, not of those who see. They are dead, not of those who are alive. They present to God their self-devised law and presume to limit His infinite powers and deem Him weak. So they shall be dealt with according to their condition.

When you stand up in prayer, it is necessary for you to have firm faith that your God has power over all things. Only then will your prayer be accepted and you will behold the wonders of God's power that we have beheld. Our testimony is based on observation and not on hearsay. How should the supplication of a person be accepted and how should he have the courage to pray at times of great difficulty, when according to him he is opposed by the law of nature, unless he believes that God has power over everything? O fortunate ones, follow not these practices. Your God is One who holds aloft innumerable stars without the use of columns and who has created heaven and earth from nothing. Then would you think so ill of Him as to imagine that your objective is beyond His power?[1] Such ill-thinking will frustrate

---

[1] God is incapable of nothing. Nonetheless, with regards to prayer, the Book of God sets out the principle that He deals with pious people most mercifully like a friend; at times, He overlooks His own will in order to accept their prayer, as He says Himself: * ادْعُونِي أَسْتَجِبْ لَكُمْ. However, at times, God desires that His own will be done, as He says: ** وَلَنَبْلُوَنَّكُمْ بِشَيْءٍ مِّنَ الْخَوْفِ وَالْجُوعِ. Thus, on occasion, God deals with a person according to the supplicant's prayer because He wishes to enhance their certainty and enlightenment. And on other occasions, He carries out His own will so that he may confer upon man the

you. Our God possesses countless wonders, but they are visible only to those who become His out of sincerity and loyalty. He does not disclose His wonders to those who do not believe in His Power and who are not sincere and loyal to Him. How unfortunate is the man, who even now, is unaware that there is a God who has power over all things. Our paradise lies in our God. Our highest delight is in our God for we have seen Him and found every beauty in Him. This wealth is worth procuring though one might have to lay down one's life to procure it. This ruby is worth purchasing though one may have to lose oneself to acquire it. **O ye, who are deprived! Hasten to this fountain as it will satiate you.** It is this fountain of life that will save you. What am I to do? How shall I impress the hearts with this good news? What sort of a **drum** am I to beat in the streets in order to make the **announcement** that this is your God, so that people might hear? What remedy shall I apply to the ears of the people so that they should listen?

If you become one with God, rest assured that God too will be yours. God Almighty shall remain awake for you as you sleep. God shall watch over your enemy and frustrate their designs,

---

robe of His pleasure, to raise his station, and to enable him to advance on the path of guidance by his love. (Author)

  * Pray unto Me; I will answer your *prayer*. (*Surah Al-Mu'min*, 40:61, Publisher)

  ** And We will try you with something of fear and hunger. (*Surah Al-Baqarah*, 2:156, Publisher)

while you are unmindful of him. You still do not know the extent of God's powers. Had you known, not a single day would you have grieved over the world. Does he who owns a treasure weep, cry and become sorrowful unto death over the loss of a single coin? Had you been aware of this treasure and knew that at every time of need God is able to fulfil your requirements, why would you look to the world so restlessly? God is a **precious treasure**; appreciate Him accordingly, for He is your Helper at every step. You are nothing without Him, nor do your resources and your schemes amount to anything. Do not follow other people for they have become wholly reliant on material means. Just as a snake devours dirt, they consume the filth of inferior worldly means. They gorge themselves on carrion in the manner of vultures and dogs. They have become estranged from God. They have worshipped men, devoured the flesh of swine and consumed wine as though it were water. They have become lifeless, for they place all their reliance on material resources and do not seek the help of God. The heavenly soul has escaped their bodies as a pigeon flies from its nest. They are afflicted with the leprosy of material worship, which has consumed their internal organs. Thus, beware of this leprosy. I do not forbid you to employ material means within moderation; only that you do not become slaves to them like other nations and that you do not forget the God who is the very Provider of these means. Had you possessed insight, you would have seen that God is everything and all else is nothing. One cannot so much as stretch or fold one's arms without His will. One who is [spiritually] dead may laugh at this, but physical death would have been better for him than such ridicule. Beware! Though other nations have progressed far in their worldly designs, do not envy them and seek to follow in their footsteps. Listen and know well that they are wholly unaware and unmindful of the God who calls you to Himself. What is their god? Only a helpless mortal. Thus, they are languishing in heedlessness. I do not forbid you from the trade and business of the world; rather, I exhort you not to imitate those who have considered the world to be everything. In all that you do, whether material or religious, continue to supplicate God so that you may be granted strength and ability. Your supplications should not be confined to mere lip service, but you ought to truly believe that every blessing descends from heaven. You will become righteous only when, in every time of need or difficulty, prior to employing any plan, you shut your door and fall down at the threshold of God with your difficulty, and supplicate to Him so that He may resolve it by His Grace. You will then be helped by the Holy Spirit and a path will be opened for you from the unseen. Have mercy on your souls and do not follow those who have completely cut themselves off from God and depend wholly on material means, to the extent that they do not even seek strength from Allah by saying *Insha'Allah*.[1] May

---

[1] If Allah so wills [Publisher]

God open your eyes so that you should realise that He is the central beam of all your plans. If this beam should fall, can the rafters continue to support the roof? Indeed not, for they would suddenly fall and would perhaps even cause a loss of life. In the same way, your plans cannot succeed without the help of God. If you do not seek His assistance, and do not make it your rule to seek strength from Him, you will never achieve anything and will die in immense sorrow. Do not wonder why other nations seem to succeed, while they are not even aware of the existence of God who is your Perfect and Mighty Lord. The answer is that they have been subjected to the trial of the world on account of their abandoning God. At times, He opens the doors of the world to a person who forsakes Him and seeks the joys and pleasures of the world and runs after its riches, in order to try him. Such a one is wholly bereft and deprived in respect of religion. In the end, he dies with his mind devoted wholly to the world and is cast into an eternal hell. At other times, the trial of God is such that a person is deprived of this world as well. But this latter kind of trial is not as dangerous as the former, for the one who is subjected to the former is more arrogant. In any case, both these groups are described as those who have incurred the wrath of God.

God is the fountainhead of true prosperity. How can people attain true prosperity if they are unaware of the Ever-Living and All-Sustaining God and are ignorant and heedless of Him, and even turn away from Him? Blessed is one who understands this secret and ruined is one who does not.

Similarly, do not follow the philosophers of this world and do not be overawed by them, for they only pursue follies. True philosophy is that which God has taught you in His Word. Those who are in love with secular philosophy are in ruin and truly successful are those who have sought true knowledge and philosophy in the Book of God. Why do you follow the paths of foolishness? Will you teach God that which He does not know? Do you hasten to follow the blind so that they should guide you? **O foolish ones!** How will he, who is himself blind, guide you? True philosophy is, in reality, acquired through the Holy Spirit as has been promised. Through it you will be carried to the acquisition of pure knowledge, to which others have no access. Ultimately, you will obtain such knowledge by sincerely seeking it. Then will you come to know that this is the very knowledge which revitalises and revives the heart and guides you to the pinnacle of certainty. How is it possible to receive pure nourishment from he who feeds upon carrion? How can he who is blind help you see? All pure wisdom descends from heaven. What then do you seek from the people of this world? Those whose souls ascend to heaven are the true heirs of wisdom. He who is not satisfied himself cannot bestow satisfaction upon you, but first purity of heart is required; sincerity and purity are needed, after which, everything will be bestowed upon you. Do not think that God's revelation is a thing of the past[2] and that the Holy Spirit can no longer descend as it did so in previous times.

I tell you truthfully that all doors may close—but the one from which the Holy Spirit descends, never shuts. Open the doors of your hearts so that the Holy Spirit may enter it. By closing the window from which the ray of light enters, you distance yourself from this sun of your own accord. Unenlightened ones! Come forth and open this window so that the sun might itself enter you. God has not closed the paths of His worldly blessings in this age. Rather, He has increased them. Do you then think that the paths of the blessings of heaven, which you sorely need at this time, have been closed by Him? Most certainly not! Rather, this door is wide open. In *Surah Al-Faatihah* God has taught that the door to every single blessing of the past has been opened for you. Why then do you refuse to accept them? Thirst for this fountain and water will spring forth itself. Weep for these blessings in the way a child wails for the milk of its mother—then will milk be given to you. Become worthy of compassion so that you may be shown mercy. Be restless so that you may be put to ease. Be ceaseless in your fervent entreaties so that a hand may come to your aid. The path of God is difficult. But, it is made easy for those who throw themselves into this deep abyss, without fear for their lives. In

---

[2] The Holy Quran has perfected the Law of God, but this has not brought an end to revelation, for it is the life of a true religion. Any religion which is devoid of ongoing divine revelation is dead and forsaken by God. (Author)

their hearts, they choose fire for themselves and decide to set themselves ablaze for the sake of their Beloved. They cast themselves in fire only to discover that it is paradise. This is what God has said:

$$ وَ اِنْ مِّنْكُمْ اِلَّا وَارِدُهَا كَانَ عَلٰى رَبِّكَ حَتْمًا مَّقْضِيًّا $$ [3]

That is, O ye who do evil and o ye who do good! There is none from among you who shall not pass through the fire of Hell. But he who throws himself into this fire for the sake of God will be saved. And He who throws himself into this fire for the sake of their inner self, which incites to evil, are consumed by it. So, blessed are those who wage war with their inner selves for the sake of God. And wretched are those who war with God for the sake of their own souls, and act against His will. He who ignores the will of God for the sake of his inner self will never enter heaven. Strive hard so that not even a single dot or iota of the Holy Quran may testify against you and cause you to be punished. For even the smallest particle of evil is punishable. Time is short and there is no telling how long one shall live. Make haste—for twilight will soon descend. Consider over and over what you shall present before God, lest it be deemed so inadequate that it is no more than waste, no more than a foul and defiled offering unfit for presentation before the Royal Court.

I have heard that some among you completely reject the Hadith.

---

[3] *Surah Maryam*, 19:72 [Publisher]

41

Those who hold this opinion are grossly mistaken. I have never taught such a doctrine. On the contrary, it is my belief that there are three components, which God has bestowed on you for your guidance. First and foremost is the Quran,[4] which elaborates on the Oneness, Glory and Greatness of God and resolves disputes between the Jews and Christians. For example, it settles the difference and misconception of whether or not Jesus, son of Mary, died an accursed death on the cross, and whether he was ever spiritually exalted thereafter, as all other Prophets were. Further, the Quran forbids the worship of anything besides God—whether man, beast, moon, sun, star, material provisions or one's own ego. So beware and do not take a single step contrary to the teaching of God and the guidance of the Quran. I tell you truly that anyone who disregards even a small injunction of the seven hundred commandments of the Quran, shuts upon himself the door of salvation. The ways of true and perfect salvation have

---

[4] The second means of guidance is the Sunnah, that is, the impeccable example of the Holy Prophet, peace and blessings of Allah be upon him, which was manifested through his deeds and actions. For example, he performed the prayer and taught how it should be offered. Then, he demonstrated how to observe the fast through his own example. Thus, the Sunnah is the action of the Prophet which gave physical expression to the Word of God. This is termed as the Sunnah. The third means of guidance are the Hadith, that is, those sayings of the Holy Prophet which were collected after his demise. The status of the Hadith ranks below the Quran and Sunnah, for many Hadith are based on conjecture. But, those Hadith that are supported by the Sunnah ought to be considered authentic. (Author)

been opened by the Quran and all else is its reflection. Therefore, study the Quran with deep contemplation and hold it very dear. Love it more than anything else. God has said to me:

$$\text{اَلْخَيْرُ كُلُّهُ فِي الْقُرْآنِ}$$

Meaning, all good is contained in the Quran. This is the truth. Pity those who favour anything besides it. The fountainhead of all your prosperity and salvation lies in the Quran. There is no religious need of yours which is not fulfilled by it. On the Day of Judgement, the Quran will confirm or deny your faith. There is no other book beneath heaven besides the Quran, which can directly guide you. God has been most beneficent towards you in that He has bestowed upon you a book like the Quran. I tell you truly that if the book which has been recited to you was recited to the Christians, they would not have perished. If this favour and guidance which has been bestowed upon you had been granted to the Jews in place of the Torah, some of their sects would not have denied the Day of Judgement. Therefore, appreciate this favour that has been bestowed upon you. It is a most precious favour; it is a great wealth. If the Quran had not been revealed, the whole world would have been nothing more than a filthy half-formed lump of flesh. The **Quran** is a book, in contrast with which, all other guidance amounts to nothing. The Gospel was revealed by the **Holy Spirit**—who appeared in the form of a **pigeon**—a creature so weak and frail that it is preyed on by cats. Thus, the Christians, day by day, sank into a pit of

43

weakness until no trace of spirituality could be found in them. The entire foundation of their faith rests on a pigeon. In contrast, the Holy Spirit of the Quran appeared in such a magnificent form that it filled the entire earth and heaven with its being. How can the pigeon compare with this grand manifestation mentioned in the Holy Quran?

The Quran can purify a person within a week as long as it is followed in letter and spirit. The Quran can make you like the Prophets, so long as you do not flee from it yourself. Which other scripture, besides the Quran, gives hope to its readers from the very outset and teaches the prayer:

$$\text{اِهۡدِنَا الصِّرَاطَ الۡمُسۡتَقِيۡمَ صِرَاطَ الَّذِيۡنَ اَنۡعَمۡتَ عَلَيۡهِمۡ}^{5}$$

That is, Guide us on the path of those blessings, which the people of the past were guided on: the Prophets, the Messengers, the Truthful [*Siddeeqeen*], the Martyrs [*Shuhadaa*] and the Righteous [*Saaliheen*]. So take courage and do not reject the invitation of the Quran, for it desires to bestow upon you such blessings as were given to those before. Has He not bestowed upon you the land of the Children of Israel and their Bayt-e-Maqdas, which to this day remains in your possession?

As for those who waver in their belief and are weak-spirited! Do you believe that God has made you the physical heirs to the lands of the Israelites, yet He was unable to make you their spiritual

---

5 *Surah Al-Faatihah,* 1:6-7 [Publisher]

successors? In truth, God intends to bless you with greater favour than them. God has made you inherit their spiritual and material wealth. However, no other will be your heir until doomsday dawns. God shall never deprive you of the blessings of revelation, and divine inspiration, converse and discourse. He will complete upon you all those blessings He has bestowed on the people of the past. However, I call to witness God and His angels that he who insolently forges a lie against God and falsely claims to be the recipient of divine revelation and wrongly says that he has been blessed with divine discourse, will be destroyed. For such a person speaks untruth about his Creator and acts deceptively; he demonstrates manifest temerity and impudence. So be cautious in this respect. Cursed are those who fabricate false dreams and wrongly claim to be recipients of divine discourse, for by doing so, in their hearts they think that God does not exist. However, the punishment of God will forcefully seize them and their days of misfortune will see no end. So strive in the way of truth, piety, righteousness and progress in the personal love of God and view this as the chief objective of your life. Then, in accordance with His will, God shall bless whomsoever He pleases from among you with His discourse. But, you should not wish for such things lest a wave of satanic influence overtakes you due to selfish desire. Many are destroyed in this way. So render service and immerse yourselves in worship. All your efforts should be expended in following all the commandments of God and to progress in certainty. You ought to do this for the sake of salvation, not for the ostentatious display of revelation. There are many pure commandments in the Holy Quran, one of them being to shun all forms of idolatry, as an idolater remains deprived of the fountain of salvation. And do not tell lies for lying too is a form of idolatry.

Unlike the Gospel, which forbids one to look covetously and lustfully at women who are not *Mahram*[6] but permits it otherwise, **the Quran** instructs against glancing at women under any circumstances, be it covetously or with pure intentions because one is liable to stumble on this account. In fact, your eyes should always be lowered when you confront a *Non-Mahram*. You should not be aware of the physical form of a woman except through an obscured sight, in the way a person's vision is clouded in the early stages of cataract. Unlike the Gospel, **the Quran** does not permit its followers to drink **alcohol,** so long as they are not intoxicated by it. Rather, it **forbids** its **consumption** completely. Otherwise, you would be lost from the path that leads to God and His converse, nor would God cleanse such a person of their impurities. The Quran says that such things are the invention of Satan and **you should guard yourself against them**.

---

[6] A man or woman with whom marriage is impermissible. [Publisher]

Unlike the Gospel, **the Quran** does not only forbid you from **being angry** with your brothers without due reason. Rather, it instructs you not only to suppress your own anger but to act upon [7] تَوَاصَوْا بِالْمَرْحَمَةِ and exhort others to follow this example as well. Not only should you have mercy on others, but advise your brothers to do the same.

Unlike the Gospel, **the Quran** does not instruct you to forbear with all your wife's improprieties except in the case of adultery. Nor does it forbid divorce. Instead, it says: [8] اَلطَّيِّبَاتُ لِلطَّيِّبِينَ. In other words, the Quran does not desire for the **impure** to remain with the **pure**. Though your wife may not be adulterous, if she casts lustful glances at others and embraces them; or is guilty of such actions which verge on infidelity, though she has not yet committed the act of adultery; or if she reveals her nakedness; if she is idolatrous and mischievous; and if she is averse to the Holy God in whom you believe, then, if she does not change her ways, you are free to divorce her, for her mode of life has already estranged her from you. She is no longer a part of you. Under such circumstances it would not be lawful for you to shamelessly remain with your wife, for she is no longer a part of your body, but is instead a foul and rotten limb, which ought to be

---

[7] And exhort one another to mercy. (*Surah Al-Balad*, 90:18) [Publisher]
[8] Good things are for good men. (*Surah An-Nur*, 24:27) [Publisher]

amputated. Let it not be the case that she diseases your other limbs as well, which then causes your death.

Again, **the Quran**, unlike the Gospel, does not completely prohibit you from taking oaths. Rather, it prohibits meaningless oaths. For on certain occasions oaths are a way to bring about a judgment. God does not desire that any form of testimony be prevented—otherwise His wisdom would be brought into question.

It is only natural that when no one is available to testify in a dispute, an oath in the name of God becomes necessary because it calls upon God as a witness. And unlike the Gospel, **the Quran** does not prohibit you from resisting an **oppressor** in all circumstances. Rather, it says:

$$ جَزٰٓؤُا۟ سَيِّئَةٍ سَيِّئَةٌ مِّثْلُهَا فَمَنْ عَفَا وَ اَصْلَحَ فَاَجْرُهٗ عَلَى اللّٰهِ ^{9} $$

That is, the recompense of any injury is an injury the like thereof. But, if a person shows forgiveness and pardons another person's wrongdoing and their clemency results in reform instead of further transgression, then God is pleased with such a person and will reward him accordingly. Thus, in light of the Quran neither is punishment praiseworthy in all cases, nor is forgiveness commendable in all circumstances. Rather, it encourages the ability to judge circumstances appropriately. Any retribution or forgiveness ought to be administered in proper accordance with

---

[9] *Surah Ash-Shura*, 42:41 [Publisher]

the circumstances and with wisdom, not arbitrarily. This is the true import of the Quran. And unlike the Gospel, **the Quran** does not encourage you to love your **enemies**. Rather, it teaches you to dissolve your personal enmities and show compassion to everyone. But, those who oppose God, your Messenger and the Book of Allah are certainly your enemies. However, even then, you ought not to exclude them from your prayers and supplications. Oppose their actions, not their persons, and seek to rectify their deeds. For God says:

اِنَّ اللّٰهَ يَأْمُرُ بِالْعَدْلِ وَالْاِحْسَانِ وَ اِيْتَآئِ ذِى الْقُرْبٰى ¹⁰

That is, God desires of you no more than that you deal equitably with all people and show kindness even to those who have not done you any good. More importantly, you ought to love God's creation as if it were your kith and kin, in the same manner that mothers treat their children. In acts of goodness there resides a concealed element of vanity. And every so often people tend to boast of their favours to others. But such a person who performs goodness out of spontaneous desire, in the likeness of a mother, can never be concerned for vanity. Thus, the highest level of virtue originates from one's natural yearning, like that of a mother. Moreover, this verse not only relates to God's creation but also to God Himself. Justice *[Adl]* towards God means to

---

¹⁰ *Surah An-Nahl*, 16:91 [Publisher]

49

remember His blessings and show obedience to Him. Goodness *[Ihsaan]* towards God means to be so firmly convinced of His existence as though one can see Him. And [11] اِیْتَآئِ ذِی الْقُرْبٰی [to give like the giving of kindred] before God can be defined as worship that is not adulterated by the greed of paradise or the fear of hell. For even if it was supposed that neither paradise nor hell existed, this would not affect your zeal, love and obedience toward Him.

The Gospel states that you should seek blessings for those who curse you. However, the Quran teaches that you should do nothing of your own ego. Rather, acquire an edict from your heart—the abode of divine manifestations—on how to govern your behaviour toward such persons. If God instils in your heart that the one who curses you is worthy of compassion and is not cursed by heaven—curse them not. Thus, you will not stand in opposition to God. But, if your conscience does not exonerate them and it is instilled in your heart that they are cursed by heaven, do not seek blessings for them. None of the Prophets sought blessings for Satan nor did they seek to liberate him from his curse. However, do not act rashly in cursing another. For many an ill-thought is steeped in falsehood and many a curse recoils on the curser. Mind your every step and deliberate over your actions and seek assistance from God, for you are blind. Or else, you might consider a just person to be a tyrant or one who is

---

[11] Ibid.

truthful to be a liar and thereby displease God. In this way all your good deeds will be wasted.

Similarly, the Gospel instructs that you should not perform good deeds so that they should be seen by others. But, the Quran admonishes against concealing all your actions from others. Instead, when wisdom dictates, perform certain actions secretly when you deem it better for your soul, and display certain actions when you believe they will benefit others in general. Thus, you will have two rewards, and as a result of your actions, those weaker people who find it difficult to muster the courage to commit good acts, might be inspired to follow your example. God himself has elaborated on the wisdom of this teaching in His Word by saying [12] سِرًّاوَّعَلَانِيَةً. That is to say, do good works both secretly and openly. This means that not only should one counsel others verbally but encourage by example as well. Mere words are not always adequate in every situation; one's practical example often has a greater impact on others.

Similarly, the Gospel teaches its followers to supplicate in seclusion. But the Quran instructs you not to pray in seclusion on all occasions. At times you ought to openly pray before others, in the company of your brethren. For, if any of your entreaties are accepted, they might serve to increase the faith of the gathering at large and cause others to be inclined towards prayer.

---

[12] Secretly and openly (*Surah Al-Baqarah*, 2:275) [Publisher]

Similarly, the Gospel directs us to pray: 'Our Father which art in heaven, hallowed be thy name. Thy kingdom come, thy will be done in earth, as it is in heaven. Give us this day our daily bread. And forgive us our debts, as we forgive our debtors. And lead us not into temptation, but deliver us from evil. For thine is the kingdom, and the power, and the glory for ever.'[13]

Contrary to this, the Quran says that the earth is not empty of God's Holiness, for it is proclaimed not only in heaven, but also on earth. As it is said:

$$وَ اِنْ مِّنْ شَیْءٍ اِلَّا یُسَبِّحُ بِحَمْدِہٖ \quad {}^{14}$$

$$یُسَبِّحُ لِلہِ مَا فِی السَّمٰوٰتِ وَمَا فِی الْاَرْضِ \quad {}^{15}$$

That is, every particle of heaven and earth glorifies and proclaims the Holiness of God and everything in them is engaged in His glorification and praise.

The mountains remember Him, the rivers remember Him, the trees remember Him and many righteous people are occupied with His remembrance. Anyone who does not remember Him with his heart and tongue and does not humble himself before God is humbled by diverse types of torment and chastisement, as a result of divine decree. According to the Book of God, angels display the highest degree of submission. The same is true of each

---

[13] *Matthew 6:9-13* [Publisher]

[14] *Surah Bani Israa'eel,* 17:45 [Publisher]

[15] *Surah Al-Jumu'ah,* 62:2 [Publisher]

and every leaf and particle in the earth, as stated in the Holy Quran. Everything is obedient to Him; not even a leaf can fall without God's command. No medicine can heal without His command, nor can any food provide nourishment without it. Everything prostrates itself at the threshold of God with extreme humility and submission and is engrossed in subservience to Him. Every particle of the earth, the mountains; every droplet of the rivers, the oceans; every leaf of all the trees and plants, including their every element; every particle of man and beast recognise God, obey Him and extol His praise and glory.

That is why Allah the Exalted has said:

$$ يُسَبِّحُ لِلّٰهِ مَا فِى السَّمٰوٰتِ وَمَا فِى الْاَرْضِ ^{16} $$

That is to say, everything in the earth glorifies Allah and proclaims His Holiness, as does everything in heaven.

Then how can it be said that God is not praised and glorified in the earth? One who possesses complete understanding could never utter such a thing. Among the things of the world some are made obedient to divine laws and others are subject to divine decree, while others still are bound to the obedience of both. The clouds, wind, fire and earth are all immersed in the obedience and glorification of God.

A person who disobeys the commandments of divine law is still

---

[16] Ibid.

bound by the orders of divine decree. No one is beyond the realm of these two dominions. Everyone is bound to the heavenly kingdom in some form or other. It is true that on account of the purity and corruption of human hearts, heedlessness and divine remembrance prevail in the earth by turns, but God has not willed for this ebb and flow to occur arbitrarily, but in accordance with divine wisdom. Just as night follows day, periods of guidance and impiety alternate according to the law and will of God, not by themselves. Despite this, everything hears His voice and extols His holiness. But the Gospel says that the earth is empty of the glorification of God. This prayer of the Gospel goes on to state that the Kingdom of God has not yet arrived on the earth. Due to His dominion not yet having been established on earth, God's will has not been put into effect on the earth, as it operates in heaven. The teaching of the Quran, however, is altogether contrary to this. The Quran clearly states that no thief, murderer, adulterer, disbeliever, or anyone who is disobedient, rebellious or an offender can perpetrate any evil upon the earth unless he is permitted from heaven. So, how can it be said that the Kingdom of Heaven does not yet prevail on earth? Does some other opposing force stand in the way of the enforcement of God's command on the earth? **Holy is Allah!** Certainly not.

Rather, God Himself has established one law for the angels in heaven and another one for man on the earth. In His Kingdom of Heaven, God has given no choice to the angels. Obedience is inherent in their very nature. They are unable to disobey. They are not subject to error or forgetfulness. But human nature has been given the choice to accept or reject. Since this freedom has been conferred from on high, it cannot be said that the presence of a transgressor threatens the Kingdom of God. God's Kingdom reigns supreme in every respect. Nonetheless, there are two systems of law. One law of divine decree governs the angels in heaven, and this makes it impossible for them to commit sin, while another law of divine decree governs the people of the temporal world and gives them the choice of good and evil from on high. But when a person seeks strength from God for the power to overcome evil, then with the support of the Holy Spirit he becomes able to conquer his weakness and safeguard himself from committing sin, as is the case with the Prophets and Messengers of God.

In the case of those who have been guilty of sin, asking for forgiveness can deliver them from the consequences of sin and they are spared from chastisement, for when light arrives, darkness is dispelled. Those evildoers who do not beg for forgiveness, that is to say, who do not seek strength from God, continue to suffer punishment for their offences. In these days, the plague has also descended upon the earth as a punishment and claims the lives of those who transgress against God. Then how can it be said that the Kingdom of God has not been established on earth?

Do not be misled by the thought that if the Kingdom of God is present on earth then why do people commit sin? Sins are also subject to the divine law of decrees. Thus, even though such people put themselves outside the law of religion, they cannot escape divine providence, that is to say, the law of divine decree. Then how can it be said that sinners do not bend to the yoke of the divine kingdom?

In British India today, theft and murder are rampant, and criminals of every class, such as those who are guilty of adultery, fraud and embezzlement etc., lurk within the State. But, it cannot be said that the British government does not rule over this land. Although the government is still in power, it has deliberately decided against executing a harsh law that would terrorise its subjects, thus making their lives unbearable. For, if the State desired, it could easily throw everyone guilty of crime into prison, thus easily preventing them from criminality; or, introduce harsher punishments, thus putting an end to crime. Hence, you can appreciate that the current rate at which alcohol is consumed, the increase of prostitution, and occurrences of theft and murder are not because the British government does not rule this land. Rather, the leniency of the government's law has facilitated the proliferation of crime and not because the British government has abdicated its authority. As a matter of fact, it is well within the power of the State to pass a more stringent law and prescribe severer punishments in order to prevent crime. Such is the example of a human government, which is of no value in comparison to the Kingdom of God. Then how great and powerful is the Kingdom of God. If the divine law was to become so oppressive that every adulterer were to be struck by lightning, and every thief were to be afflicted by a disease whereby his hands would become rotten and fall away, and every rebellious one who denies God and His religion were to die of the plague, then before the passing of a week, the whole world would put on the garment of righteousness and virtue. Thus, the Kingdom of God is surely established on earth, but heavenly law has bestowed this much freedom that evildoers are not immediately seized with punishment. Nevertheless, punishments are meted out as well: earthquakes occur; lightning strikes; volcanoes erupt violently and claim thousands of lives; vessels sink; hundreds of lives are lost in railway accidents; storms rage; houses are reduced to rubble; some are bitten by snakes; wild beasts tear apart others; epidemics break out; and not one, but thousands of doors of destruction are open, which God's law of nature has established in order to punish offenders. Then how can it be said that God's Kingdom **has not** been established on earth?

There is no doubt that His Kingdom definitely reigns supreme. Every wrongdoer has shackles around their wrists and chains around their feet, but divine wisdom has softened its law to a degree that these shackles and chains do not manifest their constraints immediately. However, if man persists in his wrongdoing, they carry him to eternal hell and cast him into such torment, in which a wrongdoer neither lives nor dies.

In short, there are **two** systems of law, **one** which relates to the angels, in that they have been created for obedience alone, with their obedience being characteristic of their bright nature. They cannot sin, but they cannot progress in virtue either. The **second** system of law relates to human beings, in that, by their nature, they can be guilty of sin, but they can also make progress in piety. Both these natural laws are unchangeable and as an angel cannot become human, so too a human cannot become an angel. Both these systems of law are unchangeable—they are eternal and immutable. The law that operates in heaven cannot operate on earth, nor can the law that operates on earth be made applicable in respect of angels. If human faults end in **repentance**, man can become much better than angels, for angels lack the capacity to make progress. Human sins are forgiven through repentance. Divine wisdom leaves some individuals free to commit sin so that thereby they should become aware of their weakness and may be forgiven through repentance. This is the law which has been prescribed for man and this is what best accords with man's nature.

Error and forgetfulness are characteristics of human nature, not of the angels. How can the law which regulates angels be applied to human beings? It is an error to attribute any weakness to God Almighty. These are merely the consequences of the law that are manifested upon the earth. Is God so weak that His Kingdom and power and glory are limited to heaven alone, God-forbid, or is it that some other deity possesses authority over the earth? The Christians should not emphasise that God's Kingdom operates **only in heaven** and has not yet been established on earth, for they hold that heaven is nothing. It is apparent that if heaven, where God's Kingdom should operate, is nothing, and God's Kingdom has not yet arrived upon earth, this would mean that His Kingdom does not rule anywhere. We observe with our own eyes that God's Kingdom is in operation on the earth. According to His law, our lives come to an end and our conditions change continuously. We experience hundreds of types of comfort and pain. Thousands of people die by God's command and thousands are born, prayers are accepted, signs are manifested and the earth produces thousands of varieties of vegetables, fruits and flowers by His command. Then does all this occur without the Kingdom of God? Rather, heavenly bodies seem to follow a chartered course at all times and no apparent change or alteration is perceived in respect of them, which should indicate the existence of a being who brings about change in them. The earth, however, is continuously undergoing thousands of changes, alterations and transformations. Every day tens of millions of people depart this world and tens of millions are born. In every way and respect the control of a Powerful Creator is felt. Is there still no Kingdom of God on earth?

The Gospel puts forward no reason why the Kingdom of God has not yet arrived on earth. Albeit, the Messiah did pray for deliverance all through the night in the garden [of Gethsemane] and, as it is recorded in Hebrews 5 verse 7, his supplication was accepted as well, yet despite this, God did not have the power to deliver him! This, according to the Christians, could possibly serve as an argument to affirm that at the time there was no Kingdom of God on earth. But I have experienced greater trials and **have been delivered** from them. How then **can I deny** the Kingdom of God? Was the case in which I was, at the instance of Martyn Clarke, charged with conspiracy to murder in the court of Captain Douglas so that I would be sentenced to death, less grave than the case which was brought by the Jews against Jesus in the court of Pilate, merely on account of religious differences and not because of any charge of murder? But as God is the Sovereign of both heaven and earth, He informed me in advance of this case in that such a trial was forthcoming and then He told me that I would be exonerated. This news was announced to hundreds of people in advance and ultimately I was discharged. It was the Kingdom of God which delivered me from this case which had been brought against me at the joint instance of the Muslims, Hindus and Christians. Thus, not once, but many a time, I have witnessed the Kingdom of God upon earth and I am compelled to believe in the verse:

لَهُ مُلْكُ السَّمٰوٰتِ وَ الْاَرْضِ ۱۷

Meaning, the Kingdom of God is established both upon earth and in heaven. Moreover, I am bound to believe in the verse:

اِنَّمَآ اَمْرُهٗٓ اِذَآ اَرَادَ شَيْئًا اَنْ يَّقُوْلَ لَهٗ كُنْ فَيَكُوْنُ ۱۸

That is, all of heaven and earth is obedient to Him. When He wills a thing He says 'Be' and it happens at once. Then God says:

وَاللّٰهُ غَالِبٌ عَلٰٓى اَمْرِهٖ وَلٰكِنَّ اَكْثَرَ النَّاسِ لَا يَعْلَمُوْنَ ۱۹

In other words, God has full power over His will, but most people are unaware of His power and might.

So much for the prayer taught in the Gospel which causes human beings to despair of the mercy of God and allows Christians to take exception with His providence, beneficence, reward and punishment to the extent that they consider God incapable of helping them in this world, until His Kingdom should arrive upon the earth. In contrast, the prayer that God has taught the Muslims in the Quran illustrates that God is not powerless on the earth, like vanquished rulers. On the contrary, His system of providence, graciousness, mercy, reward and punishment are in operation on earth and He has the power to help those who worship Him and can destroy sinners with His wrath. **The prayer** is as follows:

---

[17] *Surah Al-Hadeed,* 57:3 [Publisher]
[18] *Surah Yaaseen,* 36:83 [Publisher]
[19] *Surah Yusuf,* 12:22 [Publisher]

اَلْحَمْدُ لِلّٰهِ رَبِّ الْعٰلَمِيْنَ ـ الرَّحْمٰنِ الرَّحِيْمِ ـ مٰلِكِ يَوْمِ الدِّيْنِ ـ
اِيَّاكَ نَعْبُدُ وَ اِيَّاكَ نَسْتَعِيْنُ ـ اِهْدِنَا الصِّرَاطَ الْمُسْتَقِيْمَ ـ
صِرَاطَ الَّذِيْنَ اَنْعَمْتَ عَلَيْهِمْ ـ غَيْرِ الْمَغْضُوْبِ
عَلَيْهِمْ وَ لَا الضَّآلِّيْنَ ـ
اٰمِيْن ـ[20]

Translation: God alone is worthy of all praise. That is to say, there is no deficiency in His Kingdom. None of His excellences await a future state, which is deficient today, but would be supplemented tomorrow. No aspect of His Kingdom is ineffectual. He nourishes all the worlds. He bestows His mercy prior to any endeavour. Further, He also bestows His mercy in response to man's actions. He rewards and punishes at the appointed time. Him alone do we worship and from Him alone do we seek help. We pray that He should show us all the paths from which we can earn His bounty and should keep us away from those paths which would incur us His wrath and lead us astray.

This prayer which is set out in *Surah Al-Faatihah* is in clear contrast to the prayer taught in the Gospel, which rejects the present Kingdom of God as having been established on earth. Thus according to the Gospel neither, God's providence, nor His graciousness, nor His mercy, nor His power to reward and punish is in operation on earth because God's Kingdom has yet to be

---

[20] *Surah Al-Faatihah*, 2:2-7 [Publisher]

established on earth. *Surah Al-Faatihah,* however, indicates that God's Kingdom is present on earth and this is why the *Surah* fully illustrates all the requisites of kingship.

It is obvious that a king should possess the following qualities: he should possess the ability to nourish the people. In *Surah Al-Faatihah* this quality is alluded to with the words **Rabb-ul-Aalameen** [Lord of all the Worlds]. The second quality of a king should be that he should arrange for all the necessities that are required for the sustenance of his subjects, out of his kingly mercy and not in return for any service. This quality is affirmed in God by referring to Him as **Ar-Rahmaan** [the Gracious]. The third quality, which a king should possess is that he should appropriately help his subjects towards the achievement of that which they cannot attain by their own efforts. The *Surah* affirms this quality by the use of the word **Ar-Raheem** [the Merciful]. The fourth quality that a king should possess is that he should have the power to dispense reward and punishment so that social conditions should not be disturbed. This quality is affirmed in God by describing Him as **Maaliki Yaumid-Deen** [Master of the Day of Judgement]. In short, the aforementioned *Surah* presents all those essentials of kingship, which prove that God's Kingdom and kingly control are in operation on earth. As such, God's *Ruboobiyyat* [providence] is present, His *Rahmaaniyyat* [graciousness] is present, His *Raheemiyyat* [mercy] is present, His ongoing succour and punishment are present; indeed, all the prerequisites of kingship are found to existent on earth, in relation to God. Not a single particle is beyond His authority; every kind of recompense and each and every form of mercy rests in His hand.

On the other hand, the Gospel teaches that the Kingdom of God has not yet been established among us and that we should pray for its future establishment. In other words, at present, their God is not the master and king of the earth. Thus, how can one invest any hope in such a God? Listen and understand that true cognizance is to know that every particle of the earth is as much under the control of God as every particle of heaven is within His Kingdom. Both heaven and earth display a grand manifestation. As a matter of fact, the manifestation of heaven is a matter of faith. The average person has neither ascended to heaven nor witnessed this manifestation, but the manifestation of God's Kingdom upon earth is clearly visible to everyone's eyes.[21]

Every human being, however wealthy he might be, must ultimately drink from the goblet of death, contrary to his desire. Observe, therefore, how the manifestation of the command of

---

[21] The verse, *وَحَمَلَهَاالْإِنْسَانُ also establishes that only human beings are capable of true obedience to God, for they are able to elevate their obedience to a state of love and affection. They take upon themselves thousands of trials and prove that God's Kingdom reigns on earth. How can the angels render the kind of obedience that is coupled with anguish of heart? (Author)

*But man bore this trust. (*Surah Al-Ahzaab*, 33:73, Publisher)

this true King is visible upon the earth, for when His commandment comes, no one can ward off their death for even a second. When a person is afflicted with a vile and mortal illness, no medical practitioner or physician is able to cure it. Reflect, therefore, what a manifestation of God's Kingdom can be seen on earth in that His command cannot be rejected. How then can it be said that the Kingdom of God is yet to be established on earth and will arrive at some time in the future?

Reflect therefore that in this age, God's heavenly commandment has shaken the earth with the plague so that this may serve as a sign for His Promised Messiah. Who then can remove it without God's will? How can we assert that God's Kingdom has not been established on earth? An evildoer dwells on God's earth like a captive and seeks to evade his death, but God's true kingdom brings about his end and the angel of death ultimately seizes such a person. How then can it be suggested that the Kingdom of God is yet to be established on earth? Take heed! Every day millions of people die on earth in a moment by God's command and millions more are born in accordance with His will. Millions of underprivileged persons are made wealthy by His command and millions of the wealthy become poor. Then how can it be said that God's Kingdom has not yet been established on earth?

Heaven is inhabited by the angels alone, but on earth, there are both men and angels, who are the agents of God and servants of His Kingdom. They guard the various enterprises of man, and are constant in their obedience to God and send their reports to Him. Then how can it be said that the Kingdom of God is yet to be established on earth?

As a matter of fact, God has been recognised with most clarity by His earthly kingdom for everyone imagines that the secret of heaven is hidden and cannot be witnessed. And so in the present age most Christians and their philosophers have rejected even the existence of heaven, on which the Gospels base the whole Kingdom of God. The earth, however, is actually a temporal abode, where thousands of divine decrees are manifested. This enables us to understand that all this change, transformation, birth and death occurs by the command of an extraordinary Master. Then how can it be said that the Kingdom of God has not yet been established on earth? Such a teaching is most inappropriate in an age when the Christians have vigorously denied the existence of the heavens. For this prayer of the Gospel readily admits that the Kingdom of God has not yet been established on earth, whilst on the other hand, all Christian scholars have, on the basis of modern study, concluded in their heart of hearts that heaven is of no importance and does not exist. As a result of this, God is left with neither His Kingdom on earth, nor in heaven. The Christians reject the heavens, while their Gospel denies the earthly Kingdom of God. Now, according to the Christians, God neither holds authority over the kingdom of this world nor over that of heaven.

In *Surah Al-Faatihah,* however, our God who is the Lord of Might and Glory, has specified neither heaven nor earth and has thus disclosed to us the reality by saying that He is **Rabb-ul-Aalameen** [the Lord of all the Worlds]. That is to say, wherever habitations[22] or creatures of any kind exist, whether bodies or souls, God is the Creator and Sustainer of all. He is constant in His sustenance and provides for them according to their needs. His constant providence, graciousness, mercy, and punishment and reward are in operation perpetually at all times and in all the worlds. Let it be borne in mind that the phrase **Maaliki Yaumid-Deen** [Master of the Day of Judgement] in *Surah Al-Faatihah* does not simply mean that reward and punishment would be awarded only on the Day of Judgement. The Holy Quran has repeatedly and explicitly stated that the Day of Judgement will be the time of **the Grand Recompense.** However, one type of punishment and reward begins in this very world, which is indicated in the verse:

$$ \text{يَجْعَل لَّكُمْ فُرْقَانًا}^{23} $$

Let it also be known that the prayer of the Gospel seeks daily bread as is stated in the words: 'Give us this day our daily bread.' How peculiar to think that such a one should be able to provide

---

[22] The compound *Rabb-ul-Aalameen* is such a complete term that even if it was discovered that other habitats existed within the celestial bodies elsewhere, they too would be encompassed by this. (Author)

[23] He will grant you a distinction. (*Surah Al-Anfaal,* 8:30) [Publisher]

bread, when His rule is still to be established on earth. For, at present, all the fields and fruits grow independently of His command and rain falls without His influence. What power does He possess to bestow anyone bread? One should ask of Him to provide bread, only after His Kingdom has been established on earth, for at present he has **no influence** over anything of this world. It is only after He assumes full control over this dominion that He can grant bread to anyone. At present, even to implore Him is inappropriate. Then, the subsequent statement: 'And **forgive us** our debts, as we have forgiven those who are indebted to us,' is also incorrect in this respect. After all, what debt is owed to God when He has no dominion over the world yet and the Christians have gained nothing from His hand? No debt needs to be cleared with such an empty-handed God, nor need He be feared, for His Kingdom has yet to be established on earth, and the authority of His sovereignty is unable to inspire even the least bit of awe. What power has He to punish a sinner or destroy a people by the plague, as did He the transgressing people of the era of Moses^{as}; rain stones upon them as was done with the people of Lot; or eradicate the disobedient by an earthquake, lightning or some other chastisement, while God's Kingdom **has not even been established on earth?** Thus, as the God of the Christians is as frail as His **son** and as dispossessed as His son, it is futile to offer supplications to Him imploring: **'forgive us our debt.'** What debt did we owe Him to begin with so that He should forgive us it, for His **earthly kingdom** is yet to be established? Since His Kingdom has not even been established on earth this would imply that all the growth in the world is independent of His command and all things of earthly nature do not belong to Him; rather, they are self-existent because He has no dominion over the earth. And because He is not the King and Sovereign of the world and none of its comforts are by His royal dictates, He has no authority or right to punish anyone. It is therefore **absurd** to take such a feeble one to be God and still invest hope that he will intervene in the workings of the world, for His Kingdom is yet to be established on earth. In contrast, the prayer of *Surah Al-Faatihah* teaches us that on earth, God possesses at all times the same **power** that He possesses over other worlds. In the very outset, *Surah Al-Faatihah* speaks of those perfect and mighty attributes of God which have not been so clearly stated by any other scripture in history. As Allah the Exalted states, He is *Ar-Rahmaan* [Gracious], He is *Ar-Raheem* [Merciful] and He is *Maaliki Yaumid-Deen* [the Master of the Day of Judgment]. Thereafter, we are taught to beseech Him. In addition, the supplication in question does not merely ask for daily bread like the prayer taught by the Messiah. Instead this prayer appeals to all those faculties which human nature has been endowed with since eternity and for all that it has been made to thirst after; and that is:

اِهۡدِنَا الصِّرَاطَ الۡمُسۡتَقِیۡمَ صِرَاطَ الَّذِیۡنَ اَنۡعَمۡتَ عَلَیۡهِمۡ [24]

That is, O Master of these perfect attributes; O the Munificent one who nourishes each and every particle, all of which **benefit** from Your grace, mercy and power to reward and punish! Make us heir to the pious people of the past and bestow on us each and every blessing that You bestowed on them. And save us from disobedience lest we incur Your wrath and protect us lest we are deprived of Your help and are thereby led astray. *Aameen.*

Now by this entire discourse, the difference between the prayer of the Gospel and the prayer of the Quran has become evident. The Gospel merely promises that the Kingdom of God will come, whereas the Quran says that the Kingdom of God is with you. Moreover, not only is it present, but everyone already practically reaps the advantages of its beneficence. Hence, the Gospel only makes a promise. The Quran however, does not make a mere promise; but rather speaks of an established kingdom and demonstrates its bounties. The superiority of the Quran is evident from the fact that it presents a God who is the **saviour and comforter** of righteous people in this very worldly life. There is not a soul which is devoid of His beneficence, in fact, the bounty of His providence, graciousness and mercy encompasses every soul according to its needs. Conversely, the Gospel speaks of a God whose dominion is still to be established on earth, and

---

[24] Guide us in the right path—the path of those upon whom Thou hast bestowed Thy blessings (*Surah Al-Faatihah*, 1:6-7) [Publisher]

in fact, only makes a promise thereof. Now contemplate, which of the two does reason lead us to believe is more worthy of following? Hafiz Shirazi is true when he says:

مرید پیرِ مغانم زمن مرنج اے شیخ   چراکہ وعدہ تو کردی واو بجا آورد [25]

The Gospels praise the forbearing, mild, meek and those who remain passive in the face of harassment. But the Quran does not advise that one should remain meek in every circumstance, nor to refrain from confronting evil. Rather, it teaches that forbearance, humility, meekness and passivity are all meritorious, but not when exercised inappropriately. All good deeds ought to be performed with an appreciation of appropriate time and circumstance. An act of piety exercised at an inappropriate time or situation is a sin. As you are aware, rain is an invaluable and essential bounty, but if it is unseasonal, the very same causes devastation. You know well that one cannot maintain their health by exclusively eating either cold foods or hot foods. You can only maintain your health by altering your diet according to various needs and requirements. Thus, sternness, clemency, forgiveness, retribution, blessing or curse, and all other forms of morality which possess benefit for you in various circumstances, also require a similar change.

---

[25] *Why do you resent me sir for I am a follower of my master,*
Although you made promises, it was he who fulfilled them. [Publisher]

Become a forbearing and kind person of the highest order but not in unreasonable and inappropriate circumstances. Along with this, it should also be remembered that truly sublime virtues— those that are unadulterated by the poison of selfish desires—are bestowed from on high by the Holy Spirit. You cannot attain these lofty morals simply through your own endeavours until they are bestowed upon you from heaven. And anyone who is not blessed with virtue through heavenly grace, which comes from the Holy Spirit, is false in their claim to possess good morals. These people may be likened to such water, which at its depth is contaminated by substantial amounts of filth and excrement, which surfaces in the heat of selfish passions. Thus, always seek strength from God so that you may be cleansed of this filth and excrement, and so that the Holy Spirit may inculcate within you true purity and beauty. Remember that true and pure morals are but one of the miracles of the righteous, in which they have no equal. Those who are not lost in God are not bestowed strength from on high. Therefore, it is impossible for them to inculcate pure morals. So establish a sincere relationship with your God. Discard all ridicule, mockery, rancour, foul language, greed, falsehood, unchastity, casting lustful glances, sinful thoughts, materialism, arrogance, pride, self-conceit, mischief and obduracy. Then will you be bestowed everything from heaven. Until you are strengthened by that heavenly power which raises you, and until the Holy Spirit, which bestows life, does not enter you, until then, you are immensely frail and plunged in darkness. In fact, you are dead and devoid of life. In such a state, neither can you contend against any misfortune nor can you escape pride and arrogance when in a position of prosperity and wealth; and you are in every way overcome by Satan and your own ego. Your only real effective remedy is that the Holy Spirit, which specially descends from the hand of God, should turn your face towards virtue and righteousness. Become the **children of heaven**, not the **children of earth.** And become the heirs of light, not those who are infatuated by darkness, so that you might escape the paths of Satan. Satan is ever concerned with the night and not with the day, for he is an experienced thief and steps forth only in darkness.

Surah Al-Faatihah is not just a mere teaching, but also contains a grand prophecy. That is to say, God has described His four attributes: *Ruboobiyyat* [providence], *Rahmaaniyyat* [graciousness], *Raheemiyyat* [mercy] and *Maalikiyyat-e-Yaumid-Deen* i.e. the power to reward and punish; and after elaborating upon His all-encompassing omnipotence, God then teaches the following prayer in the subsequent verses:

'Our Lord! Make us heirs to the pious Prophets and Messengers of the past. Open for us their path and bestow on us the blessings that were bestowed on them. Our Lord! Protect us from becoming like those people upon whom your punishment descended in this very life, i.e. like the Jewish people in the time of Jesus the Messiah, who were destroyed by the plague. Our Lord! Protect us from becoming like those people who were not guided by You and were thus led astray in the manner of the Christians.'

Hence, this prayer contains an underlying prophecy that there would be some from among the Muslims who will become heirs of the past Prophets on account of their truth and sincerity, and will be bestowed with the blessings of prophethood and messengership. And also that others would become like the Jews and punishment would descend upon them in the present life; while others still would cloak themselves in the garb of the Christians. The unchangeable custom discernible in God's Word is that when a certain people are forbidden from committing a certain act, as per the knowledge of God, some from among them will commit it, whereas others will choose righteousness and virtue. Since the remotest ages, it has been the eternal practice of God that whenever He reveals a book in which He forbids a nation against an evil act or urges towards a good act, He knows for certain that some people will obey while others will not. And so, the chapter under discussion prophesied that someone from among this Ummah will appear in the perfect manner of Prophets so that the prophecy derived from the verse صِرَاطَ الَّذِيۡنَ اَنۡعَمۡتَ عَلَيۡهِمۡ [1] may be perfectly and comprehensively fulfilled.

---

[1] *Surah Al-Faatihah,* 1:7 [Publisher]

fulfilled. Then, a group from among this Ummah are bound to appear, who shall be like those Jews who were cursed by Jesus and then afflicted by the punishment of God so that the prophecy contained in the verse [1] غَيْرِ الْمَغْضُوبِ عَلَيْهِمْ may be manifested. Another group still from among them will become like the Christians who, on account of their drunkenness, moral permissiveness, sinfulness and immorality were left deprived so that the prophecy expounded in the verse [2] وَلَا الضَّالِّينَ may be fulfilled.

It is part of the doctrine held by the Muslims that in the Latter Days, many thousands of 'so-called' Muslims will come to resemble the Jews. This has been prophesied in the Holy Quran at many an instance. Moreover, one can easily notice and observe that thousands of Muslims are either converting to Christianity or choosing to live entirely free and unrestrained lives like those of the Christians. In fact many such people who are still referred to as Muslims prefer the Christian way of life. Despite their being referred to as Muslims, they hold a strong aversion towards prayer, fasting and the injunctions which relate to lawful and unlawful matters. It can be seen that both these classes of people, who have become like the Jews and Christians, are prevalent in this country. Thus, the two aforementioned prophecies of *Surah Al-Faatihah* have been fulfilled before your very eyes. One can observe how the Muslims have come to resemble the Jews and

---

[1] Ibid.
[2] Ibid.

have donned the garb of the Christians. Therefore, the third part of the prophecy is also worthy of being readily accepted. For just as the Muslims would imitate the Jews and Christians and partake of the unrighteousness found to exist within them, there was bound to be others from among the Muslims who would be entitled to achieve the rank and status of those holy personages of the Children of Israel who once lived. To entertain that God referred to the Muslims as Jews and Christians because they followed the evil ways of both, yet entirely deprived this Ummah from attaining the rank of their past Prophets and Messengers, is to think ill of God Almighty. In these circumstances how is one to consider this Ummah as the very best? Rather, it would be the worst Ummah, for it would have adopted every evil but missed out on every virtue. Is it not necessary that someone from among this Ummah should appear as a Prophet or Messenger and be the heir and reflection of all the Prophets of the Children of Israel? It is far from the mercy of God Almighty that he should raise in this Ummah thousands of persons in this age who possess the characteristics of the Jews and allow thousands more to convert to Christianity and yet not raise a single person who would be the heir of the past Prophets and partake of their blessings. It is necessary that the prophecy contained in the verses,

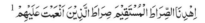

---

[1] Guide us in the right path—the path of those upon whom Thou hast bestowed Thy blessings (*Surah Al-Faatihah,* 1:6-7) [Publisher]

be fulfilled just like the already fulfilled prophecy, which states that the Muslims would become like the Jews and Christians. This Ummah has been given thousands of terrible names and it is evident from the Holy Quran and the Hadith that they were also destined to become like the Jews. Thus, in such circumstances, in keeping with the grace of God, it was only essential that where the Muslims took on the evils of the past Christians, they should have also inherited that which is virtuous. It is for this reason that in the following verse of *Surah Al-Faatihah,* [1] اِهْدِنَا الصِّرَاطَ الْمُسْتَقِيْمَ God Almighty proclaimed the good news that some people from among this Ummah would be bestowed the same blessings as the Prophets of the past. They were not destined to solely adopt the bad habits of the Jews and Christians while completely forgoing their virtues.

It is this very point which has also been indicated in *Surah At-Tahreem,* that some people from among this Ummah would resemble Mary the Truthful, who lived a life of chastity. Then, the soul of Jesus was breathed into her womb and he was born to her. This verse signifies that someone from among this Ummah would first be conferred the station of Mary and then the soul of Jesus would be breathed into him. Then would Jesus emerge from Mary. That is to say, the attributes of the person who resembles Mary would be transformed into those of Jesus. In other words,

---

[1] *Surah Al-Faatihah,* 1:6 [Publisher]

the quality of being Mary's likeness would give birth to one who takes on the form of Jesus. In this way such a person would be referred to as 'the Son of Mary'. Thus, in *Barahin-e-Ahmadiyya,* I was first given the name Mary, as can be inferred from the revelation on page 241: [1] اَنّٰی لَکَ ھٰذَا. That is, O Mary! Wherefrom did you attain this blessing? A revelation on page 226[2] also makes reference to this: ھُزِّ اِلَیۡکِ بِجِذۡعِ النَّخۡلَةِ. That is, O Mary! Shake the trunk of the palm tree. And then on page 496 of *Barahin-e-Ahmadiyya* the following revelation is present:

یَا مَرۡیَمُ اسۡکُنۡ اَنۡتَ وَزَوۡجُکَ الۡجَنَّةَ نَفَخۡتُ فِیۡکَ مِنۡ لَّدُنِّیۡ رُوۡحَ الصِّدۡقِ

That is, O Mary! Enter heaven with your companions. I have breathed into you from Myself the Soul of Truth. In this revelation God has referred to me the Soul of Truth. This is a reference to the verse [3] نَفَخۡنَا فِیۡهِ مِنۡ رُّوۡحِنَا. Thus, in this instance, the soul of Jesus is metaphorically referred to as having been breathed into the womb of Mary and named the Soul of Truth. Finally on page 556 of *Barahin-e-Ahmadiyya* a revelation was received about the birth of that Jesus who was once in the womb of Mary. It is as follows:

[1] English readers may refer to *Barahin-e-Ahmadiyya* (English translation), p. 208, Islam International Publications, 2014 Ed. [Publisher]
[2] English readers may refer to *Barahin-e-Ahmadiyya* (English translation), p. 199, Islam International Publications, 2014 Ed. [Publisher]
[3] We breathed into him of Our Spirit. (*Surah At-Tahreem,* 66:13) [Publisher]

يَا عِيْسَى إِنِّيْ مُتَوَفِّيْكَ وَرَافِعُكَ إِلَيَّ وَجَاعِلُ الَّذِيْنَ اتَّبَعُوْكَ

فَوْقَ الَّذِيْنَ كَفَرُوْا إِلٰى يَوْمِ الْقِيَامَةِ.[1]

Here, I have been named Jesus and the revelation discloses the fact that the Jesus who was breathed into Mary as referred to on page 496 has appeared. So, in this respect, I have been named Jesus son of Mary because my status as Jesus emerged from my initial status as Mary, through the breath of God. See pages 496 and 556 of *Barahin-e-Ahmadiyya*. It is this very phenomenon of the birth of Jesus son of Mary in this Ummah, which has been vividly prophesied in *Surah At-Tahreem*, wherein it is explained that someone from among this Ummah will firstly be transformed into the likeness of Mary. Thereafter the soul of Jesus will be breathed into this Mary. As such, for a period of time this person will be nurtured in the womb of Mary before being born as the spiritual manifestation of Jesus. And in this way, such a person will come to be known as Jesus son of Mary. This is the prophecy regarding the Son of Mary who would be from among the Ummah of Muhammad[sa], which was revealed almost 1300 years ago in *Surah At-Tahreem* of the Holy Quran. Then, in *Barahin-e-Ahmadiyya*, God Almighty Himself has expounded on the verses of *Surah At-Tahreem*. The Holy Quran is with you.

---

[1] 'O Jesus, I will cause thee to die and will exalt thee to Myself, and will place those who follow thee above those who disbelieve, until the Day of Resurrection. (*Surah Aal-e-Imraan*, 3:56) [Publisher]

If one were to study the Holy Quran with *Barahin-e-Ahmadiyya* and ponder over this matter with fairness, reason and piety, one would be able to see how the prophecy in *Surah At-Tahreem*— that a person from among this Ummah would also be named Mary and would then be transformed therefrom into Jesus, i.e. be born from Mary—was fulfilled in the revelations of *Barahin-e-Ahmadiyya*. Is this within the power of man? Did I have any control over this affair? Was I present when the Holy Quran was being revealed so that I could request for a verse to be sent down which would make me the Son of Mary and thereby alleviate any future accusations relating to my being referred to as the Son of Mary?

Moreover, was it possible, that twenty or twenty-two years ago, rather, even before this, I could have crafted the plan to forge a revelation so that I may first be referred to as Mary, and then gone on to concoct a revelation which suggested that like the Mary of the past, the soul of Jesus was also breathed into me; and then finally on page 556 of *Barahin-e-Ahmadiyya* written that from Mary I had now emerged as Jesus?

My dear ones! Reflect and fear God. This is surely not the work of man. Wisdoms as profound and subtle as these transcend the understanding and judgement of man. If, long ago, during the publication of *Barahin-e-Ahmadiyya*, I had plotted such a thing, why then would I have written that the Messiah, Jesus son of Mary will descend to return from heaven in the same book? For

God knew that if I had knowledge of this point, my present argument would fall weakly. So although God referred to me as Mary in the third part of *Barahin-e-Ahmadiyya,* and as is evident from the treatise itself, for two years I was nurtured in the likeness of Mary and continued to develop in the cloak of secrecy. Then after two years had passed, as it is recorded in the fourth part of *Barahin-e-Ahmadiyya* on page 496, like Mary, the soul of Jesus was breathed into me, and in metaphorical terms, I was impregnated. Then, after a period of no more than ten months, through the revelation recorded towards the end of the fourth part of *Barahin-e-Ahmadiyya* on page 556, from Mary I was transformed into Jesus. And thus, I became the Son of Mary. However, God did not inform me of this hidden secret at the time of the publication of *Barahin-e-Ahmadiyya,* even though all the divine revelations in which these hidden secrets were found were sent down to me and were recorded in *Barahin.* But, I was not made aware of their meaning and sequence. As mentioned, I therefore also recorded the traditional doctrine of the Muslims in *Barahin-e-Ahmadiyya* [that Jesus will descend from heaven physically]. And this testifies to my sincere and straightforward nature. My opponents cannot hold me accountable for recording this traditional creed, which was not based on revelation because I do not claim to know anything of the unseen until it is explained to me by God Almighty Himself. Thus, in that period of my life God desired in His wisdom that part of the import of the revealed secrets recorded in *Barahin-e-Ahmadiyya* should remain beyond my under-standing.

But, when the time arrived, these secrets were revealed to me. It was then that I realised that my claim to being the Promised Messiah was nothing that had not been referred to before; rather, it was the same claim that had been repeatedly and clearly recorded in *Barahin-e-Ahmadiyya*. Here, I also wish to remark on another revelation, though I cannot recall whether it has hitherto been published in any of my previous treatises or announcements. Nevertheless, I do remember that I disclosed it to hundreds of people. This is recorded in my personal notebook of revelations. It dates back to the time when God **first conferred upon me the title of 'Maryam' and when I received revelation regarding the breathing of the spirit. After this, I received the following revelation:**

$$\text{فَأَجَاءَهَا الْمَخَاضُ إِلَى جِذْعِ النَّخْلَةِ}$$

$$\text{قَالَتْ يَالَيْتَنِي مِتُّ قَبْلَ هٰذَا وَ كُنْتُ نَسْيًا مَّنْسِيًّا}$$

That is, then the pain of delivery caused Mary; that is myself, to go towards the trunk of a date palm. In other words, I was confronted with the common masses, the ignorant, and their benighted scholars who did not possess the fruit of belief. They rejected and ridiculed her and unleashed a storm of invective. Then did Mary say: 'Would that I had died before this and become a thing forgotten.' This refers to the clamour first raised by the Muslim clerics on the whole, who found my claim to be intolerable. They exhausted every possible means to destroy me. Thus, in the above revelation, God Almighty has illustrated the pain and suffering that overwhelmed my heart as a result of the hue and cry raised by the ignorant. There are other revelations to this effect. For example:

لَقَدْ جِئْتِ شَيْئًا فَرِيًّا ـ مَا كَانَ اَبُوْكِ امْرَءَ سَوْءٍ وَمَا كَانَتْ اُمُّكِ بَغِيًّا

Related to this also is the revelation on page 516 of *Barahin-e-Ahmadiyya* as follows:

اَلَيْسَ اللّٰهُ بِكَافٍ عَبْدَهٗ ـ وَلِنَجْعَلَهٗ اٰيَةً لِّلنَّاسِ وَرَحْمَةً مِّنَّا

وَكَانَ اَمْرًا مَّقْضِيًّا ـ قَوْلَ الْحَقِّ الَّذِيْ فِيْهِ تَمْتَرُوْنَ

See the twelfth and thirteenth lines of page 516 of *Barahin-e-Ahmadiyya*.

Translation: "And the people said: 'O Mary! What a contemptible and despicable act you have committed, far from virtue. Your father[1] and mother were never like this.' But God will establish the innocence of His servant from such allegations. And, We will make him a sign for the people. This had been decreed since the

---

[1] **Note:** This revelation reminded me of Fazl Shah or Mehr Shah, a Sayyid who lived in Batala and loved my father dearly and held a close relationship with him. When he was informed that I had claimed to be the Promised Messiah, he wept profusely and said that my father was a decent man. By this he meant that I was nothing like him, for my father was a pious, honest, upright and pure-hearted Muslim. Similarly, many people suggested that by making this claim, I had blemished my family. (Author)

very beginning and it was bound to be fulfilled. He is Jesus son of Mary, but the people doubt it though this is the truth."

All this is taken from *Barahin-e-Ahmadiyya* and these revelations are actually Quranic verses which relate to Jesus and his mother. In these verses, Allah the Exalted says that the very same Jesus who was accused by the people of being an illegitimate child would be made a sign of God. This is the Jesus whom you await. The Jesus and Mary referred to in the above revelations are none other than me. It is I, about whom it has been said that God will make him a sign and I am the Jesus son of Mary whose advent was awaited and about whom they harbour misgivings. However, this is the truth and I am the one whom you await. Doubts stem merely from ignorance. Those who fail to understand God's hidden secrets and who only see what is in front of them, are unable to discern the inner truth.

Know well that one of the great objectives of *Surah Al-Faatihah* is also to teach the prayer:

اِهْدِنَا الصِّرَاطَ الْمُسْتَقِيْمَ صِرَاطَ الَّذِيْنَ اَنْعَمْتَ عَلَيْهِمْ ²

In the prayer of the Gospel while one is taught to supplicate for their daily bread, in the above prayer, all the blessings and rewards that were bestowed on the Prophets and Messengers of the past have been sought from God Almighty. It is worth deliberating

---

² Guide us in the right path—the path of those on whom Thou hast bestowed Thy blessings (*Surah Al-Faatihah*, 1:6-7) [Publisher]

over this difference. Nevertheless, just as the prayer of the Messiah was accepted and the **Christians have received their daily bread** in abundance, similarly, this Quranic prayer was accepted through the Holy Prophet, peace and blessings of Allah be upon him, and those who were pious and virtuous from among the Muslims, and **the most excellent** from among them in particular, were made **heirs** to the Israelite Prophets. In actuality, the birth of the Promised Messiah in this very Ummah is also a **fruit** of the acceptance of this very prayer. For although many saints and holy persons partook of similarities between the Israelite Prophets under the cloak of secrecy; but by the command and order of God, the Promised Messiah of this Ummah was publicly commissioned in the likeness of the Israelite Messiah so that the resemblance between the **Mosaic dispensation and that of Muhammad**[sa] be understood.

It is for this reason that the present **Messiah** has been made to perfectly resemble the Son of Mary, to the extent that this Son of Mary has been tried in the same manner as the Israelite one. Firstly, just as Jesus son of Mary was born of the very breath of God, this Messiah was also born from within Mary by the breath of God in accordance with the promise of *Surah At-Tahreem*. Moreover, just as a great uproar was raised at the birth of Jesus son of Mary and ignorant opponents said to Mary, [3] لَقَدۡ جِئۡتِ شَیۡئًا فَرِیًّا, so too was my case as a vehement uproar was raised against me.

---

[3] Thou hast brought forth a strange thing (*Surah Maryam*, 19:28) [Publisher]

Furthermore, when the Mary of the Israelites gave birth to her son, God responded to the allegations of her opponents with the following proclamation regarding Jesus:

$$^1\text{وَ لِنَجْعَلَهُ اٰيَةً لِّلنَّاسِ وَ رَحْمَةً مِّنَّا وَ كَانَ اَمْرًا مَّقْضِيًّا}$$

God Almighty responded to my opponents with the **very same answer** in *Barahin-e-Ahmadiyya* at the time of my spiritual birth, which has been described in metaphor. God made clear to my opponents saying, 'Your machinations can do him no harm and I shall make him **a sign of mercy** for the people.' And this was destined by Him since the beginning. Similarly, the Jewish scholars issued an edict of disbelief against Jesus, which was prepared by a mischievous Jewish scholar and endorsed by other priests. Even the Jewish scholars and priests of Bayt-ul-Maqdas, most of whom were Pharisees and who numbered in the hundreds, put their seals of attestation on this edict of disbelief against Jesus.[2] This is exactly what happened with me. Then, after this edict had

---

[1] And *We shall do so* that We may make him a sign unto men, and a mercy from us, and it is a thing decreed (*Surah Maryam*, 19:22) [Publisher]

[2] Although there were many Jewish sects in the time of Jesus, peace be upon him, there were two which were considered to be true. i) Those [Saduccees] who adhered to the Torah and collectively sought verdict pertaining to religious matters from it; ii) the Pharisees were the other sect, who considered the oral tradition to be an authority over the Torah. The Pharisees were largely spread throughout the Jewish territories and followed numerous oral traditions that mostly contradicted and conflicted with the accounts of the Torah. Their argument was that certain juridico-religious matters, such as acts of worship, civil transactions and penal law were not found in the Torah, but

been issued against Jesus, he was greatly harassed. Terrible abuse was hurled at him, and offensive and defamatory books were published against him. **The same** happened to me. After 1800 years, it was as if the very same Jesus and the very same Jews had been born again. Alas, this was the meaning of the prophecy [1] غَيْرِ الْمَغْضُوبِ عَلَيْهِمْ which God had explained beforehand. But, these people were not content until they became like the Jews and incurred the wrath of God. One of the similarities between Jesus and I was **established** by the hand of God Himself when He raised me as **the Messiah of Islam** precisely at the head of the

---

were instead addressed in the oral account of the Talmud, which contained traditions from all the past Prophets. For quite some time these traditions were passed on verbally and were only recorded much later. For this reason, numerous fabricated traditions found way into the canon. In that era, since the Jews had split into 73 sects, each with its own recorded traditions, scholars of the oral tradition began to pay scant regard to the Torah and it was the oral tradition that was primarily followed, so much so that the Torah was cast aside and left abandoned. If it happened to coincide with the oral tradition, they accepted it, otherwise they did not. Thus, it was in such an age that Jesus, peace be upon him, was raised, and the chief audience of his message were the Pharisees who honoured the oral traditions over the Torah. It had been prophesied in the scriptures of the past Prophets that when the Jews would fragment into various sects and follow traditions rather than the book of God, a judge and arbiter would be given to them who would be referrd to as the Messiah; the Jews, would reject him and ultimately, a great chastisement would fall upon them, and that chastisement was the plague. We seek refuge with Allah! (Author)

[1] Those who have not incurred *Thy* displeasure (*Surah Al-Faatihah*, 1:7) [Publisher]

fourteenth century, just as He had raised the previous Messiah son of Mary at the head of the fourteenth century. God continues to show many powerful signs in my favour. And there is no one under the canopy of heaven from opposing Muslims, Jews and Christians etc., who possesses the power to match these signs. After all, how can a weak and lowly human contend against God? I am a foundation stone set by God Himself. Whosoever shall try to break this stone will be thwarted. Instead, when it falls on them, they will be crushed, for this stone belongs to God and it has been laid by the hand of God. And the second stone has been prepared and put forth in contestation by my opponents. In their opposition towards me they followed in the footsteps of the Jews of the past to the extent that they even sought my end by bringing a murder case against me, of which God forewarned me.

This case against me was far graver than the one brought against Jesus son of Mary, for the case against Jesus was based merely on a theological disagreement, which in the eyes of the ruler was of little importance; rather, it equated to nothing. However, the case crafted against me was one of attempted murder. During the Messiah's trial, Jewish priests testified against him, therefore, it was but necessary that certain Muslim clerics testified against me also. And so for this task, God chose Maulvi Muhammad Husain Batalvi. He arrived to provide his testimony draped in a long cloak in the same manner that the High Priest came to testify in court against the Messiah, and have him put to the cross. The only difference between the two was that the High Priest was given the right of a seat in the court of Pilate, as was the norm for respected Jewish personalities under the Roman government. In fact, some of them were even appointed honorary magistrates. Therefore, the High Priest was provided with a seat as per the rules of the court, while the Messiah son of Mary was made to stand like a common criminal in court. However, during my trial, the exact opposite occurred. That is to say, contrary to the hopes of my opponents, Captain Douglas, who took the place of Pilate as presiding judge in my case, allowed me to be seated. Hence, this Pilate proved himself far more virtuous than the Pilate of the Messiah son of Mary. For, in issuing his verdict, he courageously and stringently remained committed to the rules of the court and paid no heed to any external pressure, nor was he prejudiced by religion or ethnicity. He held court so impeccably that if his person was held up as a means of pride for the nation and as an example for his fellow judges, it would be entirely justified. To pass fair judgment is a difficult task. Unless one breaks off all their ties they cannot rightly fulfil the duties of this office. But I can honestly testify that **this** Pilate faithfully discharged his duty—whereas the first Pilate of Rome was unable to fulfil his duty so faithfully. His cowardice led to great hardships for the Messiah. Thus, this difference ought to always be remembered by our community for as long as the world exists and as the community grows into the hundreds of thousands and millions, this noble judge will be fondly remembered. It was his good fortune that God chose him for this task. It must be extremely trying for a judge to confront two parties, one of whom is a missionary for his religion and the other holds a belief that is at variance with his own, especially when the judge has been informed that the latter holds stark religious differences. But this courageous Pilate resiliently took on this test, despite the fact that he was shown passages from my books, which owing to a lack of erudition, were interpreted as unduly hostile to Christianity. But, despite this opposing effort, his facial expressions remained impassive, for his enlightened conscience had already arrived at the truth. And because he pure-heartedly sought the truth behind the case, God helped him and revealed upon his heart the truth, and as a result the reality was disclosed to him. He was gladdened for having been able to find the path of justice. Indeed, it was only due to his fairness that he gave me a seat just as was given to the plaintiff. But, when Maulvi Muhammad Husain came to provide his testimony against me in the way that the High Priest had testified, he found that I was seated. As such, his eyes did not look upon me in the state of disgrace that he so desired. At this, he thought to himself that equal treatment would have to suffice and so he requested a chair for himself from our Pilate. However, he reprimanded him and loudly proclaimed that **neither he nor his father** had ever been given the right of a chair [in any government institution] and that there was no official instruction to provide him a seat. The difference ought to be noted that the earlier Pilate due to his fear of the Jews offered a chair to some of the revered among them who came as witnesses, while keeping the Messiah standing, who had been presented as a criminal, despite the fact that he was sincerely well-intentioned towards him, rather, he may even be likened to a disciple. In fact, his wife was a particular devotee of the Messiah and was renowned for her saintliness. But so unnerved was he by his fear that he unjustly handed over this innocent Messiah to the Jews. Unlike myself, he was not even accused of murder, only a minor religious dispute existed. However, this Pilate of Rome was not strong of heart and was frightened by the threat that he would be reported to Caesar.

A further parallel between the Roman Pilate and this Pilate is worth remembering here. When the Messiah son of Mary was brought before the court, the earlier Pilate said to the Jews that he saw no wrong in him. Similarly, when the Messiah of the Latter Days, that is myself, was presented before the Pilate of this age, he asked that he be given a few days to prepare his defence to this charge of murder, but the Pilate of this age said: 'I accuse you not of anything.' The verdicts of both Pilates were exactly the same. If there is a difference, then only inasmuch that the earlier Pilate was unable to stand by his conviction. When Pilate was threatened with being reported to Caesar he grew apprehensive and despite knowing the truth, gave the Messiah over to the bloodthirsty Jews even though he and his wife were both perturbed by this decision for they were both strong believers of the Messiah. But, when confronted by the fury and outrage of the Jews, cowardice got the better of him. Nevertheless, he did make great attempts in secret to have the Messiah delivered from death on the cross and he was successful in this effort as well, but only after the Messiah was first hung on the cross and due to immense pain was overcome by a death-like swoon. In any case, ultimately through the efforts of the Pilate of Rome, the life of the Messiah son of Mary was saved. And for his deliverance, the prayer of the Messiah had already been accepted—see Hebrews chapter 5 verse 7.[1] After this, the Messiah secretly left this land and migrated towards Kashmir and it is here that he passed away.

As has previously been mentioned his tomb is situated in Mohalla Khanyar, Srinagar. All this was on account of Pilate's efforts. But, nevertheless, the endeavours of this earlier Pilate were tainted somewhat by cowardice. After stating that he found no sin in the Messiah, Pilate could have easily released him for he had the

---

[1] The Messiah himself had also prophesied that the only sign that would be shown would be the sign of Jonah. Thus, the Messiah indicated in this statement that just as Jonah entered into the belly of the whale alive and had escaped alive, so too would he enter the tomb alive and emerge alive. The only way that this sign could have been fulfilled was for the Messiah to have been taken off the cross alive and then taken to his tomb whilst still alive. The Messiah's declaration that no other sign would be shown refutes those who say that one of the signs that the Messiah manifested was that he ascended to the heavens. (Author)

power to do so. However, he was subdued by the threat of being reported to Caesar. In contrast, the Pilate of this age stood firm against the uproar of the clergy. This land too is ruled by an imperial power. But the Empress of today is infinitely better than the Caesar of the past. Therefore, it was not possible for anyone to pressurise the judge into forgoing justice by threatening to report him to the Empress. In any case, the Messiah of this age was subject to greater intrigue and uproar than the Messiah of the past. My opponents and the leaders of all communities came together. But the Pilate of this age gave preference to the truth and stood by his word to me that he did not find me guilty of murder. Thus, he acquitted me in a very straightforward and courageous manner. While the first Pilate was forced to employ schemes in order to save the Messiah, this Pilate dutifully fulfilled his obligations of court and all without the slightest tinge of cowardice. On the same day that I was acquitted, a thief belonging to the Salvation Army was also brought for trial. This was so because a thief was tried alongside the first Messiah as well. However, the thief apprehended along with the Messiah of the present age was not hung on the cross, nor did he have his bones broken like the first, rather, he was only given a three month prison sentence.

Let me return to my principal subject and state that *Surah Al-Faatihah* is so replete with verities, subtleties and insights that if all of them were put to writing, it would be impossible to record them in a single tome. Reflect only over the meaning of the insightful prayer, [2] اِهۡدِنَا الصِّرَاطَ الۡمُسۡتَقِيۡمَ taught in this chapter. This prayer possesses a fully-encompassing meaning, which is the key to all spiritual and worldly goals.

We can never know the true essence of anything, nor derive benefit from it, until we discover a straight path to reach it. The affairs of the world are intricate and complex, whether they relate to the responsibilities associated with kingship and administration, whether they relate to combat or battle and warfare, whether they relate to the subtleties of natural science and astronomy, whether they relate to the method of diagnosis and treatment in the field of medicine, or whether they relate to trade or agriculture. Success in any of these fields is difficult, rather well-nigh impossible to come by until one finds a clear avenue of approaching the subject at hand. When confronted by difficulty, any intelligent person compels himself to ponder night and day, for hours on end, so as to devise a means by which to resolve the problem at hand. All professions and inventions, or any other intricate and complex matter, can only be undertaken once the right approach has been adopted. Thus, in order to achieve success in worldly or religious objectives, the most effective prayer is that of seeking the right path. When one approaches anything from the correct avenue, then with the grace

---

[2] Guide us in the right path (*Surah Al-Faatihah,* 1:6) [Publisher]

of God, such a person undoubtedly can succeed in attaining their goal. God, in His power and wisdom, has set out a proper way of achieving everything. For example, no ailing person can be efficaciously treated until an effective approach for the identification and diagnosis of their ailment is followed, and the heart is lead to believe that the proposed course of action shows promising signs of success. In fact nothing in the world can be achieved until the correct method is undertaken for that purpose. And so one who strives towards an objective must first discover the correct way of achieving it. Thus, just as one first requires a correct path so as to attain success in worldly matters, so too, since time immemorial, in order to become a friend of God, and to receive His love and grace, a correct path has always been required. Therefore, in the very beginning of *Surah Al-Baqarah*, the chapter that follows *Surah Al-Faatihah*, God says: [3] هُدًى لِّلْمُتَّقِيْنَ, which means, 'the path to attain blessings is the one which We put forth.'[4]

Thus, the supplication [5] اِهْدِنَا الصِّرَاطَ الْمُسْتَقِيْمَ is a complete prayer that draws the attention of an individual to the fact that in a time of worldly or spiritual difficulty, the first thing man is obliged to

---

[3] *Surah Al-Baqarah*, 2:3 [Publisher]

[4] In *Surah Al-Faatihah* one prays for guidance toward the right path, while in the second chapter the right path is elaborated as an expression of the acceptance of this prayer. (Author)

[5] Guide us in the right path (*Surah Al-Faatihah*, 1:6) [Publisher]

seek out is the straight path which leads to the acquisition of one's objective. That is to say, they ought to search for an unclouded and straight path to achieve their goal without hindrance; so that the heart becomes full of certainty and is freed from doubts. However, in accordance with the instruction of the Gospel, **one who supplicates for bread** would not set out in search of God, for the goal of such a person is to receive bread. When this goal is achieved, what use have they for God? This is the very reason why the Christians have deviated from the right path and have adopted a most shameless belief of taking a mere mortal for God. We cannot understand what the Messiah son of Mary possessed over others by virtue of which the thought arose that he ought to be deified. Most Prophets who appeared prior to him were greater as far as miracles were concerned, such as Moses, Elisha and the Prophet Elijah. And I swear by God in whose hand is my life that if the Messiah son of Mary had lived in my age, he could never have done the things which I can do, nor could he have shown greater signs than those which are being manifested by me,[1] and he would have found that God has

---

[1] The reader will soon be able to verify this with the publication of *Nuzul-ul-Masih,* ten parts of which have already been printed and will soon be distributed. This book has been written in response to Pir Mehr Ali Shah Golarhvi's work, *Tanbur-e-Chishti'ai.* In *Nuzul-ul-Masih* it has been proved that Pir Sahib plagiarised a treatise of the late Muhammad Hasan and committed so many disgraceful mistakes that once they are exposed his life will

blessed me more than he. Now, when I occupy such a status, just think of **the rank occupied by the Holy Messenger[sa] in whose servitude I have come.**

ذٰلِكَ فَضْلُ اللّٰهِ يُؤْتِيْهِ مَنْ يَّشَآءُ [1]

In matters such as these there can be no room for jealousy or envy. God does what He wills. One who opposes the will of God is not only thwarted in their endeavours, but after their demise they are sent to hell. Ruined are those who have taken a mere mortal for God. Ruined are those who have not accepted a divinely chosen Prophet.

Blessed are those who have recognised me. Of all the ways that lead to God I am the last, and of all His lights I am the last. Unfortunate is one who rejects me, for besides me there is nothing but darkness.

The second means of guidance given to Muslims is **the Sunnah**, that is, the practical example of the Holy Prophet, peace and

---

turn bitter. As for the unfortunate Muhammad Hassan, he died in accordance with my prophecy recorded in *I'jaaz-ul-Masih*. And now the other unfortunate one, [namely Pir Mehr Ali Shah] has become another victim of the prophecy, اِنِّیْ مُهِیْنٌ مَنْ اَرَادَ اِهَانَتَكَ *

فَاعْتَبِرُوْا یٰۤاُولِی الْاَبْصَارِ **

[*So take a lesson, O ye who have eyes!*] (Author)

* I shall disgrace him who seeks to dishonour you. [Publisher]

** [*Surah Al-Hashr, 59:3,* Publisher]

[1] That is Allah's grace; He bestows it upon whomsoever He pleases (*Surah Al-Maa'idah,* 5:55) [Publisher]

blessings of Allah be upon him, which he demonstrated to elucidate the teachings of the Holy Quran. For example, the number of *Rak'aat* in the **five daily** prayers are not apparently evident in the Holy Quran. How many *Rak'aat* are to be observed in the morning and how many at other times? However, this has been clarified by the Sunnah. One ought not to be deceived into thinking that the Sunnah and Hadith are one and the same thing. The Hadith were collected after some one hundred to one hundred and fifty years, but the Sunnah existed along with the Holy Quran since the very beginning. After the Holy Quran the greatest favour that has been bestowed on the Muslims is the Sunnah. The obligations of God and His Messenger were two primarily. Firstly, God revealed the Quran and through the agency of His Word informed His creation of His will. This was the obligation of God's law. Then, the obligation of the Messenger of Allah, peace and blessings of Allah be upon him, was to practically demonstrate the Word of God and thus clearly expound it to the people. In this way he provided a practical demonstration of this Word and through his Sunnah i.e. his way of practice, the Messenger of Allah, peace and blessings of Allah be upon him, resolved matters of intricacy and difficulty. It would be wrong to suggest that such issues were resolved by the Hadith, for Islam had already been established on earth before the Hadith had come into existence.[1] Prior to the compilation of Hadith, did the people not observe prayers; or for that matter, pay the Zakat, perform the Hajj, or possess knowledge of that which was lawful or forbidden? Of course, it is true to say that the third means of **guidance are the Hadith**, for many matters relating to Islamic history, morality, and jurisprudence are elaborated on by the Hadith. Moreover, the greatest benefit of the Hadith is that they serve the Quran and Sunnah. Those who fail to properly honour the Quran proclaim that the Hadith are an authority over the Quran, just as the Jews claimed in relation to their own traditions.

But I declare that the Hadith serve the Holy Quran and the Sunnah. And it is obvious that servants only add to the grandeur of their master. The Quran is the Word of God and the Sunnah is the practice of the Messenger of Allah. The Hadith are an additional testimony in support of the Sunnah. It is wrong to suggest that the Hadith are an authority over the Quran, **God forbid**. If there is a judge that sits over the Quran, it is the Quran itself. The Hadith which are based somewhat on conjecture can never sit as a judge over the Quran; they only serve as supporting testimony. It is the Quran and Sunnah, which have provided all

---

[1] The *Ahl-e-Hadith* refer to both the sayings and actions of the Messenger to be Hadith. Whatever their terminology, the fact remains that the Sunnah was promoted by the Holy Prophet himself and is entirely separate from the Hadith which were compiled after his lifetime. (Author)

the necessary guidance, whereas the Hadith serve only as a supporting testimony. How can the Hadith be a judge over the Quran? The Quran and Sunnah were imparting guidance in an age when this man-made adjudicator did not even exist. Do not say that the Hadith are an authority over the Quran, rather consider them a reinforcing testimony to the truth of the Quran and Sunnah. Though the Sunnah expounds the purport of the Quran and is the path unto which the Holy Prophet, peace and blessings of Allah be upon him, guided his Companions through his practical example, the term does not refer to those sayings that were recorded in books after approximately one hundred to one hundred and fifty years, for these sayings are referred to as Hadith. **The Sunnah** is the practical example of those pious Muslims which has been a part of their characters since the very beginning and which thousands of Muslims have been taught to follow. Although a large part of the Hadith is based on conjecture, but so long as they do not contradict the Quran or Sunnah, they are worth accepting. For the Hadith not only support the Quran and Sunnah, but are also valuable material on various issues that relate to Islam. Therefore, to disregard **the Hadith** would be to sever off one of the limbs of Islam. However, if there is a Hadith which contradicts the Quran and Sunnah, or contradicts a Hadith which accords with the Quran; or if, for example, there is a Hadith which opposes *Sahih Bukhari,* then such a Hadith ought to be rejected. To accept such Hadith is to deny not only the Quran, but also all those other Hadith that accord with the Quran. I trust that no righteous person could show such audacity so as to accept a Hadith which contradicts the Quran, Sunnah and other Hadith which conform with the Quran.

Nevertheless, one ought to honour the Hadith and derive benefit from them, for they are attributed to the Holy Prophet, peace and blessings of Allah be upon him. Do not reject them unless the Quran and Sunnah reject them; rather, follow the Hadith of the Holy Prophet so diligently that there should be nothing you do, or do not do, except that you have a basis for it in the Hadith. But if a Hadith clearly contradicts the accounts given in the Holy Quran, one should reflect so that it may be reconciled—perhaps the apparent incongruity is the fault of your own understanding. However, if the discrepancy cannot be resolved, then any such Hadith ought to be discarded for it cannot be from the Messenger, peace and blessings of Allah be upon him. On the other hand, if there is a weak Hadith, but it conforms to the Quran, then accept it, because it stands endorsed by the Quran. And if there is a Hadith containing a prophecy, which is considered inauthentic by experts of Hadith, but the prophecy contained in it is fulfilled, either in your lifetime or from before, you ought to accept such a Hadith to be true and consider the scholars and narrators of the Hadith, who considered it to be weak and fabricated, as being mistaken or even liars. Hundreds of Hadith which contain prophecies are considered doubtful, fabricated, or weak by Hadith scholars. If any such Hadith happens to come true, and you refuse to accept it on the grounds that it is weak, or one of its narrators lack in piety, you will only establish your own faithlessness for having rejected a Hadith which was shown to be truthful by God. Reflect for a moment, if a thousand such Hadith existed but scholars of Hadith considered them to be weak, yet a thousand prophecies contained in these Hadith were fulfilled, would you declare all these Hadith to be weak and thus waste a thousand proofs in support of Islam? In this way, you will become enemies of Islam. Allah Almighty says:

$$فَلَا يُظْهِرُ عَلَى غَيْبِهِ أَحَدًا إِلَّا مَنِ ارْتَضَى مِنْ رَّسُوْلٍ^2$$

Thus, true prophecies can only be attributed to truthful Messengers. In such instances, is it not closer to piety to suggest that a Hadith scholar has mistakenly declared an authentic Hadith as weak, than to say that God has erroneously authenticated a false one?

Even if a Hadith is deemed inauthentic, it ought to be followed as long as it does not contradict the Quran and Sunnah, and other Hadith which corroborate the Quran. But, one should take great care when following the Hadith because many of them are fabricated as well and have created discord within Islam. Every

---

[2] He does not grant anyone ascendency over His domain of the unseen. Except him whom He chooses as *His* Messenger (*Surah Al-Jinn*, 72:27-28) [Publisher]

sect possesses narrations which are consistent with their own beliefs, so much so that, even an institution as firm and well established as the Islamic prayer, has been given various guises because of conflicting accounts found in the Hadith. Some recite *Aameen* loudly, while others recite it silently. Some recite *Surah Al-Faatihah* behind the Imam, while others think that this invalidates the prayer. Some fold their arms over their chests, others fold them over their navel. It is actually from the Hadith that these differences emanate.

$$ كُلُّ حِزْبٍ بِمَا لَدَيْهِمْ فَرِحُونَ^3 $$

Otherwise, the Sunnah only demonstrated one practice, but interpolated accounts caused a variance in practice. In this manner, a false understanding of the Hadith has been the ruin of many, including the Shiites. If they had taken the Quran as their final authority, then even *Surah An-Nur* [the chapter of light] alone would have sufficed to bestow light upon them. But the Hadith have become the cause of their ruin. Similarly, in the time of the Messiah, the Pharisee Jews[4] were ruined. For some time they had

---

3 Each party exulting over what they have (*Surah Al-Mu'minun,* 23:54) [Publisher]

[4] The Gospel very strongly rejected the views espoused by the traditions and narrations of the Talmud. These narrations were directly attributed to Moses by a series of narrators under the assumption that they were his revelations. Eventually, the Torah was eschewed completely and a study of the traditions alone became prevalent. In certain matters, the Talmud contradicted the Torah, but the Jews would give preference to the Talmud. (The Talmud, editor Joseph Barclay, London, 1878) (Author)

abandoned the Torah and as is their belief even today, they held that the oral tradition was a judge over the Torah. As such, they possessed many traditions which stated that their Promised Messiah would not come until Elijah physically descended from heaven. Thus, they were gravely misled by these traditions and because of their dependence on them, were unable to accept the interpretation of the Messiah that John the Baptist had come in the spirit and likeness of Elijah, and as a spiritual reflection of his character.

The very reason they stumbled was because of their oral traditions and ultimately they squandered their faith on account of them. It is also a possibility that they misinterpreted the contents of these traditions, or that these narrations were subject to human interpolation. The Muslims are perhaps not aware of the fact that the Jews who rejected the Messiah were the *Ahl-e-Hadith* of their time. They raised an uproar against him, issued an edict of disbelief against him and declared him to be a disbeliever. They further slandered him by saying that he rejected the books of God because God had prophesied the second coming of Elijah, but this man sought to misrepresent the prophecy and applied to it a far-fetched interpretation without any evidence.[1] The Messiah was not only declared a disbeliever

---

[1] When the edict of disbelief was issued against Jesus, peace be upon him, Paul was also from the party that rejected him. Later, however, he promoted himself as an apostle of the Messiah. During the lifetime of the Messiah, this man was

but also a heretic, and it was said that if this man were true then the whole of the Mosaic religion was false. Such were their dark ages, for the people were misled by false traditions. So, when reading the Hadith, one ought to keep in view the fact that a people of the past—on account of their lending greater authority to the traditions over the Torah—were led to a state where they rejected a true Prophet and declared him a heretic and the antichrist.

Sahih Bukhari however, is a most blessed and valuable collection of Hadith for the Muslims. It is the very same compilation which states clearly that Jesus, peace be upon him, has passed away. Likewise, *Muslim* and other books of Hadith are also a treasury of religious knowledge and insight. It is incumbent to follow all such traditions as long as they do not contradict the Quran,

---

a strident opponent. Not one of the Gospels which are attributed to the Messiah prophesise that after him Paul will repent and become an apostle. There is little need to write about Paul's character before his conversion, for the Christians are well acquainted with it. It is lamentable that for as long as the Messiah remained in his homeland, Paul caused him great grief. Yet after his deliverance from the cross when the Messiah migrated to Kashmir, the same person entered himself amongst his disciples on the pretext of a fabricated dream, and invented the doctrine of Trinity, and declared the flesh of swine as being lawful even though it was strictly forbidden in the Torah, and also made the consumption of wine a common practice. He entered the concept of Trinity into the doctrine of the Gospel so that all these innovations would ingratiate the idol-worshippers of Greece. (Author)

Sunnah or those Hadith which are in accordance with the Quran.

You who are in search of God! Pay heed to me and listen. There is nothing like certainty. It is certainty which delivers one from sin. It is certainty which gives you the strength to do good deeds. It is certainty which imbues you with the true love of God. Can you cease from sin without certainty? Can you cease pursuing your selfish desires without witnessing a truly certain manifestation of God? Can you discover peace without certainty? Can you bring about a sincere change without certainty? Can you achieve true prosperity without certainty? Is there beneath the heaven any atonement or expiation which can deliver you from sin? Will the so-called atonement of Jesus son of Mary grant deliverance from sin? Followers of Christ! Utter not such falsehood which brings about utter ruin on earth. Even the salvation of Christ himself was dependent on certainty. He believed with certainty and was, therefore, granted salvation. Pity the Christians who deceive others by claiming that they have received salvation through the blood of the Messiah, yet they are themselves immersed in sin from head to toe. They know not who their God truly is, and their life is spent in heedlessness. They are lost in the intoxication of alcohol, but are completely unaware of the holy inebriation which comes from heaven. They are deprived of a life of companionship with God and of the fruits borne of a holy life.

Remember, without certainty you cannot emerge from a life of darkness, nor can you find the Holy Spirit. Blessed are those who possess certainty for it is they who will come to see God. Blessed are those who rid themselves of doubt and uncertainty for it is they who shall be delivered of sin. Blessed shall you be when the treasure of certainty is bestowed upon you, for only then will your sin be effaced.

Sin and certainty cannot co-exist. Would you ever thrust your hand into a pit wherein you see an extremely venomous snake? Would you remain standing near a volcano which rains down stone? Or where lightning strikes? Or where a ferocious lion attacks? Or where a deadly plague goes on ravaging human life? If you are as certain of God as you are of the snake, lightning, lion or plague, then it would be impossible for you to disobey God and follow a course that leads to His chastisement, nor would you sever from Him your ties of sincerity and faithfulness.

You who have been called to righteousness and piety, know that you will be drawn to God and be cleansed of the vile blemish of sin only when your hearts become replete with certainty. Perhaps, some among you may say that you already enjoy certainty, but remember that you only deceive yourselves. You do not possess certainty at all because you do not possess its essentials. This is because you are still to estrange yourself from sin. Neither do you progress as you ought to, nor do you fear God in the way you ought to. Reflect for yourselves. How can a person who is certain that a serpent lies in a hole, plunge their hand therein? Similarly, he who is certain that his food is poisoned will not partake thereof. In the same manner, a person would never carelessly and heedlessly enter a jungle, if he observes with certainty that thousands of blood-thirsty lions prowl within. How can your hands and your feet and your ears and your eyes be daring enough to indulge in sin if you truly believe in God and His reward and punishment? Sin cannot overcome certainty. While you perceive a blazing and consuming fire, you would never thrust yourselves into it. The walls of certainty stretch to heaven. They cannot be scaled by Satan. It is only certainty that has ever purified anyone. Certainty strengthens one against suffering, to the extent that even kings are able to relinquish their thrones and endure the hardships of poverty. Certainty eases every type of distress. It is certainty which enables one to behold God.

All 'atonement' is false and all 'redemption' vain. All purity proceeds from the path of certainty. It is certainty alone that delivers from sin, leads to God, and puts a person ahead of even the angels in sincerity and steadfastness. Any religion that does not provide the means for attaining certainty is false. Any religion that cannot exhibit God through certain means is false. Any religion that has nothing to offer except ancient tales is false. God is as He ever was, His powers are as they always were and He has the ability to show signs as He always had. Why then are you assuaged with mere tales? A religion whose miracles and prophecies are consigned to mere fables is dead. Ruined is the community upon which God has not descended and which has not been purified by the hand of God through certainty.

Just as human beings are attracted to those delights for which their inner self yearns, so too when people experience spiritual pleasures on account of their certainty they are pulled towards God, and His beauty enchants them to such extent that everything else appears utterly meaningless. Man can only find sanctuary from sin when he comes to know with certainty of His might, punishment and reward. The root cause of all insolence is ignorance. Anyone who partakes of insight that is certain in nature cannot remain insolent. If a homeowner comes to know that a terrible flood is surging towards him, or if his property is encircled by a fire and only a small opening remains, then such a person would never remain there. How then can you claim to possess certainty in the punishment and reward of God and yet continue to remain in your terrible state? So open your eyes and look upon the Law of God that governs the entire world. Do not behave like rats who are attracted to the depths of darkness, rather, become soaring pigeons who are drawn to the sky. Do not make a pledge of repentance whilst remaining adamant on sin. Be not like the snake that sheds its skin, yet still remains a snake. Be mindful of death, for it lurks nearby though you are unmindful of it. Endeavour to purify yourselves, for only those who purify themselves can reach the Pure. But how are you to attain this blessing? God has Himself provided the answer to this, where He states in the Quran: ¹وَاسْتَعِيْنُوْا بِالصَّبْرِ وَالصَّلٰوةِ. That is, seek the help of God with patience and prayer. What is meant by prayer? It is a supplication that is humbly entreated by extolling His holiness, praise and sanctity, and seeking his forgiveness, and by invoking salutations upon the Holy Prophet. So, when you observe prayer do not recite Arabic phrases alone like those who are unmindful—for the prayer and forgiveness sought by such persons is nothing more than a superficial demonstration, which is devoid of essence; their prayers are not sustained by any foundations. When you offer your prayer, besides the verses of the Quran which are the Word of God, and besides the various prayers taught by the Holy Prophet, which are the words of the Messenger, make all your other entreaties in your native tongue so that the humility and meekness that they are born of may touch your heart.

And what are the five daily prayers? They are a reflection of your various conditions. Your life is marked by five variations in state, which overtake you in times of trial and it is essential that you experience these diverse states.

1. Firstly, when you are warned of an impending tribulation, like the issuance of a warrant in your name by the court. This is the

---

¹ *Surah Al-Baqarah*, 2:46 [Publisher]

first state which causes a decline in your peace and happiness. This state resembles your hour of decline, for as a result your contentment begins to fade. Symbolic of this is the *Zuhr* prayer, the timing of which begins when the sun begins to decline from its zenith.

2. The second change which affects you is when the time of the tribulation draws near. This may be likened to when you are apprehended as per the dictates of an arrest warrant and brought, as it were, before a judge. This is when you are overcome by fear and your blood runs cold. The light of hope and solace slowly fades away. This state resembles that part of the day when daylight grows dim and the sun can be looked at directly and it becomes clear that sunset is close at hand. This spiritual state is reflected in the *Asr* prayer.

3. The third change that overtakes you is when all hope of deliverance from tribulation seems lost. For example, when a charge-sheet is prepared against you and your opposing witnesses testify against you in order to see you perish. By this time you begin to lose control of your senses and you already consider yourself a prisoner. So this state resembles the time when the sun sets and all hope of daylight sets with it. This spiritual state is reflected in the *Maghrib* prayer.

4. The fourth change that overwhelms you is, as it were, when the tribulation finally seizes you and its deep darkness engulfs you.

For example, when you are sentenced by the judge on the basis of the charge-sheet and the testimony of the witnesses, and you are handed over to a police officer to remain in custody. This state resembles that part of the day when night finally settles and complete darkness prevails. So, this spiritual state is reflected in the *Isha* prayer.

5. Then, after you have spent a period in time engulfed by the darkness of this affliction, God's mercy finally surges forth upon you and saves you from darkness. This may be likened to when day dawns after the dark of night, and then this very light of day shines forth with all its radiance. So, this spiritual state is reflected in the *Fajr* prayer.

Thus, in view of the five states that are prevalent in the variation of your disposition, God has prescribed for you the five daily prayers. By this you can appreciate that the daily prayers are specifically for the benefit of your soul. If you desire to be safeguarded from afflictions then do not abandon the five daily prayers, for they are a reflection of your varying inner and spiritual conditions. Prayer is the cure for all future tribulations. You know not what divine decree the new day will usher in for you. So before the new day dawns, humble yourselves before your Lord, so that the new day brings for you goodness and blessing.

O you the affluent, and O Kings! O you who are wealthy! There are but few among you who fear God and are pious in the ways prescribed by Him. Most of you are devoted to the possessions and territories of this world, and spend your entire lives occupied to this end and give not thought to your death. All those wealthy persons who do not observe their prayers and are unmindful of God carry the sins of all their servants and attendants around their necks. All those wealthy persons who consume alcohol also carry the sins of the people who intoxicate themselves under their influence. You who claim to possess understanding! Know that this world is not eternal, so take hold of yourselves. Eschew all immoderation and abstain from every type of intoxicant. It is not alcohol alone that ruins a person. Opium, ganja, charas, bhang, *tarhi*,[2] and all other addictions are similarly destructive. They ruin the mind and destroy lives. So, shun all such substances. I cannot understand why one would choose to indulge in these intoxicants when, year on year, they claim the lives of thousands of addicts[3]—not to mention the torment of the hereafter.

---

[2] Opium, ganja, charas and bhang are derived from Indian hemp; *tarhi* is an intoxicating drink derived from coco, a nut water or any palm juice. [Publisher]

[3] The degree to which alcohol has harmed the people of Europe is because Jesus, peace be upon him, himself used to drink—perhaps on account of a malady or out of previous habit. But O ye Muslims! Your Prophet, peace be upon him, was **pure** and **free** from every kind of intoxicant. Indeed, he was truly free from all sin. So as Muslims who do you follow? Unlike the Gospel the Quran does not permit **alcohol**. On the basis of which scripture do you then deem alcohol to be **lawful?** Why are you so heedless of death? (Author)

Become righteous so that you may live long and receive the blessings of God. He who remains engrossed in extreme luxury, lives an accursed life. He who shows discourtesy or inconsideration, lives an accursed life. He who neglects God and is unsympathetic towards His servants, lives an accursed life. A rich person will be held accountable for their duties towards God and their fellow human beings, in the same way as will one of meagre means, nay, even more stringently. How unfortunate is one who places their trust in this short span of life and completely turns away from God and makes use of those things prohibited by God with such impudence as if they were lawful for them. In the likeness of one who is mad, when angered, such a person is prepared to curse, injure or even kill. In the heat of their lustful passions they are driven to the extremes of shamelessness. Such a person shall never attain true happiness until death seizes them.

My dear ones! You have only come to this world for a short while, much of which has already passed. Thus, do not displease your Lord. An earthly government of great might can annihilate you if you displease them. Reflect, how then is it possible for you to escape the wrath of God Almighty? If you are righteous in the eyes of God none can destroy you, for your Lord Himself shall protect you. The enemy who thirsts for your life will never be able to prevail over you. If not for this protection, no one can guard your life, and you will spend your life in fear of your enemies and be made anxious by all types of affliction. And ultimately, your final days will be consumed by grief and anger.

God becomes the refuge of those who attach themselves to Him. Therefore, hasten towards him and forgo all forms of opposition to Him. Do not be indolent in fulfilling your obligations towards Him, and do not wrong[4] His servants through your words or deeds. Remain forever fearful of the anger and wrath of heaven for **this is the only path to salvation.**

O learned ones of Islam! Do not hasten to reject me for there are many secrets which are not so easily understood. Do not reject what I have to say at the very first instance, for this is not the way

---

[4] A person who unleashes their wrath upon mankind is eventually ruined in a similar manner. That is why, in *Surah Al-Faatihah*, God has named the Jews as مَغْضُوبِ عَلَيْهِمْ [those who have incurred the wrath of God]. This implies that though all wrongdoers would incur the wrath of God on the Day of Resurrection, those who unjustly vent their rage in this world suffer by divine wrath in the present life as well. The world has not witnessed the wrath of the Christians in the same way as from the Jews. This is why in *Surah Al-Faatihah* they are referred to as *zaalleen* [the misguided]. The word *zaalleen* has two meanings. In the first instance it means they have gone astray. And in the second, it means they will be completely lost in something. I believe this is a glad tiding for the Christians as it foretells that a time will come when they will be delivered from a false religion and lose themselves in Islam. Over time they will eschew their idolatrous beliefs. They will abandon their false and disgraceful practices and become monotheists like the Muslims. Thus, the second meaning of the word الضَّآلِّينَ, which appears at the end of *Surah Al-Faatihah* means to be completely lost or immersed in something. This is a prophecy regarding the religious state of the Christians in the future. (Author)

of righteousness. If you had not been wrong about certain matters or mistaken in your interpretations of certain Hadith, the very advent of the Promised Messiah who is the Arbitrator would have been useless. A precedent has already been set, for the Jews of the past emphasised and argued the same thing that you now propose. Just as you await the second coming of Jesus, peace be upon him, they too awaited the second coming of the Prophet Elijah. They averred that the Messiah was to come only after the Prophet Elijah, who was lifted into heaven, would physically descend; and that whosoever claimed to be the Messiah prior to the coming of the Prophet Elijah was a liar. They based this belief not only on their Hadith but further quoted divine scripture— the book of Malachi—to support their claims.

But, when Jesus, peace be upon him, claimed to be the Messiah who was promised to the Jews, and Elijah did not descend, despite this apparent precondition, all these doctrines of the Jews were proven false. The belief of the Jews that the Prophet Elijah would physically come down from heaven, was ultimately understood to imply that someone else in his spirit and character would appear. Indeed, this was the interpretation put forth by Jesus himself, whom you now seek to bring down from heaven. Thus, why do you stumble at such a place where the Jews have already lost footing? Thousands of Jews reside in your country. Ask them, is their belief not exactly the same as your current belief? So why would the God who did not cause the Prophet Elijah to descend for the sake of Jesus—and he put forth interpretations to the Jews—cause him to descend for your sake? You reject the verdict of the very person whom you drag from heaven. If you are in doubt then ask any one of the many hundreds of thousands of Christians in this country, or refer to the Gospel. Did Jesus not himself aver that John the Baptist was actually the second coming of Elijah, thus dashing the hopes of the Jews? **If it is necessary in this age** that the Prophet Jesus must descend from heaven then in such a case Jesus cannot be considered a true Prophet, for if it were the established practice of Allah to send back Prophets from heaven, why did Elijah not return, and why was John declared to be Elijah on the grounds of interpretation? Those who are possessed of understanding ought to reflect on this.

Further, your doctrines that the Messiah son of Mary will descend from heaven, join forces with the Mahdi and wage war with the people in order to coerce them into becoming Muslims are such as defame the religion of Islam. Where in the Holy Quran is the use of compulsion in religious matters permitted? Rather, Allah the Exalted says in the Holy Quran: لَاۤ اِکۡرَاہَ فِی الدِّیۡنِ.[5] This means that there is no compulsion in religion. How then can the Messiah son of Mary be granted liberty to coerce people to such an extent that he would force them to either accept Islam or face death, without even accepting the *Jizyah*?

---

[5] *Surah Al-Baqarah*, 2:257 [Publisher]

In which place, part or chapter[6] of the Holy Quran is such a teaching sanctioned? The entire Quran repeatedly states that there is no compulsion in religion and evidently demonstrates that the battles which took place in the time of the Holy Prophet, peace and blessings of Allah be upon him, were not to propagate religion by force. Instead, they were in the nature of retribution, that is to say, they served as a penalty against those who had murdered a large party of Muslims and who had forced others from their homes, and committed immensely grave injustices against them. Allah the Exalted says:

$$\text{اُذِنَ لِلَّذِيْنَ يُقَاتَلُوْنَ بِاَنَّهُمْ ظُلِمُوْا وَ اِنَّ اللّٰهَ عَلٰى نَصْرِهِمْ لَقَدِيْرُ}^{7}$$

That is, permission to fight is given to those Muslims who are being subjected to war by the disbelievers, because they have been

---

[6] To suggest that it was lawful to convert the Arabs to Islam by force is a notion that is categorically rejected by the Holy Quran. However, what is established is that the whole of Arabia caused immense pain to the Holy Prophet, peace and blessings of Allah be upon him, slayed many of his companions—both men and women—and expelled from their homeland the rest who were victims of persecution. Therefore, all those who were guilty of murder, or aided in this crime, had become worthy of being slain in the eyes of God Almighty due to the bloodshed they had caused. In retribution, although they actually deserved to be slain, God who is the most Merciful of all, showed clemency by stating that their earlier crime, which made them worthy of punishment by death, would be forgiven to those of them who entered Islam. Where lies the allegation of compulsion in the presense of such mercy? (Author)

[7] *Surah Al-Hajj*, 22:40 [Publisher]

wronged, and God has the power to help them. Then, there were defensive wars, which were fought to preserve freedom of choice or to establish liberty in the land against those who aggressed to destroy Islam or forcefully suppress its propagation.

The Holy Prophet, peace and blessings of Allah be upon him, and his blessed Caliphs never waged war except in these three cases. In fact, the Muslims tolerated the injustices of other peoples to such a degree that no similar example can be found among other nations. So what right will Jesus the Messiah and the Mahdi have to come and begin murdering people? Will they not even accept *Jizyah* from the People of the Book? As a result they will abrogate the verse:

$$ \text{حَتّٰى يُعْطُوا الْجِزْيَةَ عَنْ يَّدٍ وَّ هُمْ صٰغِرُوْنَ} \text{[8]} $$

What sort of defenders of Islam will they be if upon their arrival they begin to abrogate verses of the Quran which were valid in the lifetime of the Holy Prophet, peace and blessings of Allah be upon him? And yet would such a revolution cast no blemish on *Khatm-e-Nubuwwat* [Seal of Prophethood]?

Today, after 1300 hundred years have passed since the era of the Holy Prophet, Islam has been internally divided into 73 sects. The duty of the true Messiah should be to win the hearts through argumentation, not by the sword; and break the creed

---

[8] Until they pay the tax with *their own* hand *submissively* and acknowledge their subjection (*Surah At-Tawbah*, 9:29) [Publisher]

of the cross through irrefutable and powerful arguments, rather than going about breaking crosses made of gold, silver, brass and wood. Your use of force only serves to show that you possess no argument whatsoever to support[9] your own view. Whenever an

---

[9] Certain ignorant persons, such as the editor of *Al-Manar*, level the allegation that I have only declared Jihad to be unlawful as I live under the rule of the British. What these foolish people fail to realise is that if it had been my desire to falsely please the government, why would I have stated time and again that Jesus son of Mary survived the crucifixion and died a natural death in Srinagar, Kashmir; and that neither was he God, nor the son of God? Would those from among the British who were passionate about their faith not turn away from me? You who are unenlightened! Heed what I say. I have never sought to gratify the government. The fact of the matter is that the Holy Quran forbids religious war against such a government which freely allows Muslims to engage in religious practices and traditions and does not take up the sword against us to propagate their religion. After all the government does not wage a religious war against us. It is incumbant that I express my gratitude to them, for I could not have done my work in Mecca and Medina as freely as I have in this land. The wisdom of God chose that I be born in this land. Then, am I to belittle the wisdom of God? The Holy Quran says: *وَاٰوَيْنٰهُمَآ اِلٰى رَبْوَةٍ ذَاتِ قَرَارٍ وَّمَعِيْنٍ*. In this verse Allah the Exalted explains that He saved Jesus the Messiah from crucifixion and settled him and his mother on an elevated land, which was a place of comfort with streams of running water, that is, in Srinagar, Kashmir. Similarly, God has also settled me in the elevated land of this government, where those who seek to make mischief are unable to harm me. This is an abode of peace. It is a country where streams of true knowledge flow forth, and there is peace and security against the onslaughts of those who seek mischief. Thus, am I not to be thankful for the generosity of this government? (Author)
[*Surah Al-Mu'minun*, 23:51, Publisher]

ignorant and cruel person is defeated in argumentation, they always extend their hand to seek a sword or rifle. However, a religion that can only spread its message with the help of the sword, and by no other means, can never even remotely be from God Almighty. If you do not refrain from such a Jihad and the view presented above enrages you to such extent that you should name the righteous as 'antichrist' and 'heretic,' we end our discussion on two phrases:

$$^{10} \quad \text{قُلْ يَٰٓأَيُّهَا ٱلْكَٰفِرُونَ لَآ أَعْبُدُ مَا تَعْبُدُونَ}$$

In this era of internal divide and disunity, how many people will your imaginary Messiah and Mahdi wield the sword against? Do the Sunnis not consider the Shiites worthy of being put to the sword? And do the Shiites not deem the Sunnis worthy of being utterly annihilated by the sword? Thus, when according to common belief, each sect considers the other to be liable for punishment, upon how many battlefronts will each sect fight a Jihad? But remember, God needs no sword. He will cause His religion to flourish on earth through heavenly signs and none shall be able to stop Him. And, remember that **Jesus shall never descend** again. The confession he shall make on the Day of Judgment, as mentioned in the verse [11] فَلَمَّا تَوَفَّيْتَنِي, clearly shows that

---

[10] Say, 'O ye disbelievers! I worship not that which you worship' (*Surah Al-Kaafiroon,* 109:2-3) [Publisher]

[11] Since Thou didst cause me to die (*Surah Al-Maa'idah,* 5:118) [Publisher]

He will not reappear in the world. On the Day of Judgment he will plead ignorance of the decline of the Christians. If he had returned to the world before the Day of Judgement, would he respond to God by saying that he knew nothing of the decline of the Christians? Hence, this verse demonstrates that he has clearly admitted to not returning to the world again, for if he was to come back to earth before the Day of Judgement and if he was to dwell therein for forty years, he would be uttering a lie before God Almighty by declaring that he knew nothing of the state of the Christians. What he ought to have said was that at the time of his **second advent** he witnessed almost four hundred million Christians in the world, and that he was well aware of their having gone astray, and that he was worthy of reward for converting all the Christians to Islam, and for breaking their crosses. What an utter lie it would be for Jesus to say that he had no knowledge of this matter.

In short, this verse clearly records a declaration of the Messiah which establishes that he will never return to the world. The truth is that the Messiah has passed away[1] and his grave is

---

[1] Southern Italy's most popular newspaper, the *Corriere Della Sera*, recently published a strange story:

On 13 July 1879, the elderly recluse named Kore died in Jerusalem. During his lifetime, he was renowned to be a saintly man. He left behind an inheritance. The governor sought out his relatives and handed over to them an amount of two hundred thousand francs (118,750 rupees), which was in the form of coins from different countries. They were discovered from the cave in which the recluse had lived for quite some time. Along with this money, his relatives were also handed some documents, which they were unable to read. A few scholars of Hebrew happened to view these documents and were surprised to find that these documents were in ancient Hebrew. Upon reading them the following inscription was found:

I, Peter the fisherman, a servant of Christ the son of Mary addresses the people in the name of God Almighty and in accordance with His will.

The letter ended with the words:

I, Peter the fisherman, in the name of Christ, and in my nintieth year, resolved to write these loving words, three passovers (three years) after the death of my Lord and Master, Christ the Messiah the son of Mary in Boler, near the sacred house of God.

Scholars have concluded that the script dates from the time of Peter. The London Bible Society also support this opinion and after an indepth examination of these documents have decided to purchase them from the owners for the value of four hundred thousand lire (237,500 rupees).

The prayer of Christ, son of Mary, may peace be on both of them. He said:

My Lord! I am unable to overcome that which I consider to be wrong. Nor have I attained the virtue I desired to attain. Others keep their reward in hand but I do not. My greatness lies in my work. No one is in a worser state than I. My Lord who is most high, forgive me my sins. O God, do not let it be that my enemies are able to find fault in me, nor let me be humiliated in the estimation of my friends. Let not my piety put me to trial and do not let this world become my greatest source of happiness or the chief object of my life. Do not place me at the mercy of such a one who would show me no compassion. O God, who is the most Gracious—in the name of your mercy, ordain it so. You do indeed shower your mercy on those who are in need of it. *

* (Footnote on page 69 of first edition of Urdu book) [Publisher]

situated in Mohalla Khanyar, Srinagar. [1] **Now,** God Himself shall descend and fight with those who war against the truth. God fights by manifesting His signs and there is nothing objectionable in this. However, it is definitely unacceptable for human beings to fight because they do so as an expression of physical force.

Pity these **Muslim clerics,** for if they were possessed of integrity they could have found full satisfaction by turning towards piety. And God has surely comforted those souls which are pure. But, those who were created from the same dust as Abu Jahl follow in his footsteps. A Muslim cleric from **Meerut** has sent me a notification through registered post that the *Nadwat-ul-Ulama* are holding a conference in Amritsar. He suggests that a debate ought to be held there. However, let it be clear that if my opponents had been well-intentioned and if they were not consumed by thoughts of victory and defeat, why would they have required *Nadwah* and the like to put their minds at ease? The religious scholars of *Nadwah* are, in my view, no different from those of Amritsar. They hold the same doctrines, the same character and the same disposition. Everyone is at full liberty to come to **Qadian**—not for a debate, but to hear what I have to say in order to seek the truth. If afterwards they still harbour doubt

---

[1] A Jew has also verified that the tomb in Srinagar is constructed on the pattern of the tombs of the Isrealite Prophets. See relevent note attached.**

** [Please refer to 'Appendix A']

they may seek to dispel it with humility and respect. Such people shall be considered as **guests** for as long as they remain in Qadian. I have no need to refer to the *Nadwah,* nor can they help. They are all enemies of the truth; yet, the truth continues to spread in the world. Is it not a magnificent miracle of God Almighty that twenty years before today, by way of revelation, He made evident in *Barahin-e-Ahmadiyya* that people would strive vigorously and exert their utmost efforts to bring about my failure but, ultimately, God would grant me a large community? This divine revelation dates back to a time when I did not have a single follower. Then, when my claim was published, my opponents spared no effort in their attempts against me. Ultimately, however, in accordance with the above-mentioned prophecy my community spread, and in British India to date, my community numbers more than a hundred thousand people. If the *Nadwat-ul-Ulama* are cognizant of death, they ought to consult *Barahin-e-Ahmadiyya* and the relevant official documents, and testify whether or not this is a miracle. Now when both the Quran and divine miracles have been presented to them, what purpose is served by debate?

In this country, the custodians of shrines and the descendants of saints are so estranged from religion and so deeply engrossed in their self-invented beliefs that they are entirely oblivious of the trials and tribulations that afflict Islam.

Instead of the Holy Quran and books of Hadith, their gatherings are enlivened by all sorts of tambourines, violins, drums and *Qawwali* singers etc. which are innovations in the faith. Yet despite this, they boast of themselves as being guides of the Muslims and followers of the Holy Prophet. Some of them even dress up as women, decorate their hands with henna and wear bangles. They prefer to recite poetic couplets in their congregations instead of the Holy Quran. These customs are now so deeply entrenched, they may be likened to rust, which one could hardly expect to be removed. But, God Almighty will surely manifest His powers and come to the aid of Islam.

Appendix A

[This is the English translation of the original facsimile given on the subsequent page, which appears in Ruhaani Khazaa'in, Volume 19, Kashti-e-Nuh, p. 78, Islam International Publications, 2009 Ed.]

---

*شهدشاهدمن بنی اسرئیل**

(The testimony of an Israelite scholar of the Torah
regarding the tomb of the Messiah)

'I testify that I have seen the illustration, which is in the possession of Mirza Ghulam Ahmad of Qadian, and indeed, the illustration is an accurate depiction of the tombs of the children of Israel, and of their eminent personalities. I saw this illustration on the same day that I write this testimony on 12 June 1899.'

[Signed]: *Salman Yusuf Ishaq, the trader*

'Salman the Jew wrote this testimony in my presence.'

[Witness]: *Mufti Muhammad Sadiq Bherwi,*

Clerk—Office of the Accountant General, Lahore.

'I bear witness in the name of Allah that this document was written by Salman ibn Yusuf, an eminent personality from among the Israelites.'

Signed: *Sayyid Abdullah of Baghdad*

*A witness from among the children of Israel bears witness (*Surah Al-Ahqaaf,* 46:11) [Publisher]

شہد شاہد من بنی اسرائیل

(ایک اسرائیلی عالم توریت کی شہادت دربارہ قبر مسیح)

הסערו הנד דחי דנן נרליא דן הנח בנור נודנר

میں شہادت دیتا ہوں کہ میں نے دیکھا ایک نقشہ پاس مرزا غلام احمد

דרלדח הדרהד כ'חד'יא'יב הנד דנר נחד ד ערהד דרל

صاحب قادیانی اور تحقیق وہ صحیح ہے قبر بنی اسرائیل کی قبروں میں سے

לנ ערדדל כהל מרדנד דב הד לד ודהא דל

اور وہ ہے نبی اسرائیل کے اکابر کی قبروں میں سے

הכבד'ר דב מ'ח'מדא' ווחדח דא'ה'ר נדא' דנ מרו דר

میں نے دیکھا یہ نقشہ آج کے دن جب لکھی

ו' הד'דמרד'דר' ז'דח'א' ז'נז' מ'ז'וד הד'נ'ל'ז' ז' דא'ל'

میں نے یہ شہادت بماہ انگریزی جون ۱۲ ۱۸۹۹ء

ד' ... ל' הדדח ۱۸۹۹ מר'א'י ח'א' ותרג' מוהם דרא'ור

سلمان یوسف یسحاق تاجر

ذرנد' מ'ד'ר דכ'ד'ה'ר' : ש'ל'ר'מ'ן' יהד'ר'י ני מר'י

سلمان یہودی نے میرے رو برو

ריבבו' יה שהרת' לכי מ'פ'תי מ'המד צדק

یہ شہادت لکھی ۔ مفتی محمد صادق بھیروی

ברוי כל'רך דמ'תר א'כ'יתכת' הנ'רל כ'הר

کلرک دفتر اکونٹ جنرل لاہور

اشہد باللہ ان ہذا الکتاب کتبہ سلمان ابن یوسف وانہ رجل من اکابر

بنی اسرائیل .   **دستخط: سید عبد اللہ بغدادی**

An Admonition for Women

In the present era certain **women** have also become involved in somewhat peculiar innovations in the faith. They deeply frown on the Islamic teaching of **multiple marriages**, as if they no longer consider it a part of faith. They are unaware that the Law of God contains every remedy. If the injunction of multiple marriages did not exist in Islam, such cases which compel men to enter a second marriage would remain unaddressed by the Shariah. Suppose a woman becomes insane or leprous or falls victim to any other disease which forever renders her disable or if such a circumstance arises where, although she is deserving of compassion, she loses her capacities. As the husband is also worthy of compassion since he is unable to live a life of celibacy, it would be cruel, in such a case, to the faculties of a man to prohibit him from entering into a second marriage. In actuality, it is in view of these factors that the divine law of God has left this door open for men. Similarly, in pressing circumstances, God has also opened an avenue for women. If a husband becomes incapacitated, a woman may ask a judge to allow her a *Khula,* which is also a form of divorce.

The divine law of God can be likened to a pharmacy. If the pharmacy is unable to dispense medicine for every kind of ailment, then it will not operate for long. So contemplate, is it not true that men are at times confronted with circumstances that compel them towards a second marriage? What use is a divine law that does not contain a solution for all situations?

According to the Gospel the only ground for **divorce** is adultery and the hundreds of other factors that might create severe hostility between a man and woman are ignored. Ultimately, this shortcoming has proved unsustainable for the Christian people and now, in the United States, it has become necessary that a law pertaining to divorce be enacted. So reflect, where does this law now leave the Gospel?

O women, do not despair. The book that you have been given does not require man-made amendments like the Gospel. It safeguards the rights of men just as it safeguards the rights of women. If a woman is displeased by her husband's multiple marriages, she is at liberty to seek a divorce through the authorities. If the divine law of God was ever to be considered complete, it was imperative that God furnished therein provision for all the diverse circumstances that were to confront the Muslims. O ye women, do not criticize God Almighty when your husbands intend to enter a second marriage. Rather, pray that you are protected from trials and tribulations. Undoubtedly, a husband who marries **two wives** and does not treat them equitably is most cruel and shall be held accountable. But, you on your part must not disobey God and thereby invite His wrath upon yourselves. Everyone is answerable for their deeds. If you become pious in the sight of God Almighty, your husband will be made pious also. Although religious law permits multiple marriages for men in view of various exigencies, there also exists for you the law of divine decree. If the law established by the Shariah should test your resolve then turn towards the law of divine decree through prayer. For the law of divine decree overpowers even the law of Shariah.

Become righteous and do not entirely attach your heart to this world and its attractions. Forgo your national pride and do not ridicule or mock another woman. Do not demand such things of your husbands as are beyond their capacity. Seek to enter your grave in a state that you are pure and chaste. Do not show laxity in fulfilling the obligations of God such as the prayer and Zakat etc. Be faithful to your husbands with heart and soul for much of their honour rests in your hands. So fulfil this duty with such excellence that God counts you among the virtuous and obedient. Do not be extravagant and do not be wasteful with your husband's wealth. Do not be dishonest, do not steal, do not incessantly complain and do not slander other men and women.

Conclusion

All the counsel I have written is intended to increase my community in the fear of God Almighty; and so that they become worthy of being saved from His wrath, which is currently ablaze on earth; and so that they may be saved from the plague, which is prevalent in these days. It is true piety which pleases God (**Alas! How rare is true piety).** God safeguards a truly righteous person from affliction in no ordinary way but in the manner of a sign.

Many deceitful and ignorant persons claim to be pious, but **truly pious are those** whose virtue is established by a sign from God. Anyone can claim to love God, but only those love Him, whose devotion is testified to by heaven. Everyone claims that their religion is true, but only the religion of such a one is true who is bestowed **heavenly light** in this very life. Everyone claims that they will attain **salvation,** but only such a person is true in their word who sees the heavenly light of salvation in this very world. Strive therefore, to become the **beloved** of God so that you may be saved from every affliction. A truly righteous person will be protected from the plague for they have found **sanctuary** with God. So become truly righteous. You know well what God has said regarding the plague. It is the fire of divine wrath. Save yourself from this fire. A person who sincerely follows me and is not unfaithful, indolent, unmindful, and torn between virtue and sin shall be saved. But others who tread indolently on this path and do not wholeheartedly advance in piety, or who prostrate before the world, put themselves to trial.

Show complete obedience to God in all respects. The time has now come for all those who consider themselves members of my community to sacrifice their wealth for the sake of this community as well. A person who can afford even a penny ought to donate that penny towards the expenditure of the community on a monthly basis. Those who can afford to give a rupee per month should donate a rupee every month. The costs of hospitality aside, religious projects also require substantial funds. Hundreds of guests come to visit, but comfortable guesthouses have not been built until now due to a lack of funds, though this is necessary. Sufficient bedding is not available either. The mosque requires an extension. Our print and publishing efforts lag behind our opponents. For every fifty thousand magazines and religious journals published by the Christians each month, we are barely able to consistently produce a thousand. Thus, every member of the community ought to aid such projects according to their means, so that God Almighty extends to them His help as well. It is better to consistently contribute every month even if only a small amount, than to donate after long intervals according to one's whim. Every person's sincerity is determined by their service. Dear ones! The time has come to serve religion and assist its cause. **Prize this opportunity—it shall not come again.** Those upon whom ˜˙˙˙ is liable should ˙˙˙nd their contributions here. You should all ˙˙ities and spend your wealth in this cause. Be loyal in all circumstances so that you may be blessed with favour and the Holy Spirit, for **this reward** has been prepared for those who have entered this community. The greatest manifestation of the Holy Spirit was shown to **our Prophet, peace and blessings of Allah be upon him.** At times, the Holy Spirit appeared to certain Prophets in the form of a dove, or in the form of a **cow** to other Prophets and avatars, **or in various other semblances** to others. The Holy Spirit did not manifest itself in the guise of a human being until the **advent of the perfect man,** that is to say, our Prophet, peace and blessings of Allah be upon him. When, however, the Holy Prophet, peace and blessings of Allah be upon him, appeared, since he was the perfect man, the Holy Spirit also manifested itself upon him in the form of a human being. As this powerful manifestation of the Holy Spirit encompassed the entire **breadth** of heaven and earth, for this reason, the teaching of the Holy Quran remained safeguarded against **polytheism.** Conversely, the Holy Spirit manifested itself to the **founder** of Christianity in an exceedingly **frail** form, that is, a **dove;** therefore, the unholy spirit, namely Satan, **attained ascendancy** over the religion. He exhibited his power and might in the likeness of an enormous **serpent** and assailed Christianity. This is the reason that the Holy Quran has referred to the misguidance of Christianity as being the most terrible on earth. It states that the deification of **a human as God and to attribute a son to God** is such a grave sin on earth that it could well rend heaven and earth asunder and shatter it into pieces. So, Christianity has been mentioned and refuted in the very beginning of the Quran as is understood from the verse, ¹اِيَّاكَ نَعْبُدُ and ²وَلَا

الضَّآلِّيْنَ, and then again at its close as is evident from the following:

³قُلْ هُوَ اللّٰهُ اَحَدٌ اَللّٰهُ الصَّمَدُ لَمْ يَلِدْ وَ لَمْ يُوْلَدْ

The middle part of the Quran also mentions the evil of the
Christian faith as is apparent from the verse:

⁴تَكَادُ السَّمٰوٰتُ يَتَفَطَّرْنَ مِنْهُ

Thus, according to the Quran, since the creation of the world,
creature worship and falsehood have never been so rampant as in
this age. This is why the Christians alone were called for a prayer-
duel and no other polytheists. It is not difficult to understand
why the Holy Spirit appeared in earlier times in the guise of birds
and other animals. I do point out, however, that this was an
indication of the fact that the nature of our Prophet^{sa} was so
excellent that he, as it were, compelled the Holy Spirit to appear
before him in the form of a human being. **Why do you lose heart
when you follow such a magnificent Prophet?** Display such
conduct that even the angels in heaven are left astonished at your
loyalty and purity, and invoke blessings upon you. Submit to
death so that you might be granted life. Cleanse your inner selves
of selfish passions so that God may settle in you. Completely

---

¹ Thee alone do we worship (*Surah Al-Faatihah,* 1:5) [Publisher]

² And those who have not gone astray (*Surah Al-Faatihah,* 1:7) [Publisher]

³ Say, He is Allah, the One; Allah, the Independent and Besought of all. He
begets not, nor is He begotten; (*Surah Al-Ikhlaas,* 112:2-4) [Publisher]

⁴ The heavens might well-nigh burst thereat (*Surah Maryam,* 19:91)
[Publisher]

sever your earthly ties on the one hand, and establish a perfect heavenly relationship on the other. **May God help you.**

I now conclude and pray that my teachings prove beneficial for you. May such a transformation take place within you that you become the stars of the earth, and that the earth is illumined by the light you have been granted by your Lord. *Aameen,* and again, *Aameen.*

يَا عِبَادَاللّٰهِ أُذَكِّرُكُمْ آيَامَ اللّٰهِ وَأُذَكِّرُكُمْ تَقْوَى الْقُلُوبِ ـ اِنَّهٗ مَنْ يَّأْتِ رَبَّهٗ مُجْرِمًا فَاِنَّ لَهٗ جَهَنَّمَ لَا يَمُوتُ فِيهَا وَ لَا يَحْيٰى ـ [5] فَلَا تُخْلِدُوا اِلٰى زِيْنَةِ الدُّنْيَا وَ زُوْرِهَا وَاتَّقُوا اللّٰهَ ـ وَ اسْتَعِيْنُوْا بِالصَّبْرِ وَالصَّلٰوةِ ـ [6] اِنَّ اللّٰهَ وَ مَلٰٓئِكَتَهٗ يُصَلُّوْنَ عَلَى النَّبِيِّ يٰٓاَيُّهَا الَّذِيْنَ اٰمَنُوْا صَلُّوْا عَلَيْهِ وَسَلِّمُوْا تَسْلِيْمًا ـ [7] اَللّٰهُمَّ صَلِّ عَلٰى مُحَمَّدٍ وَّ عَلٰى اٰلِ مُحَمَّدٍ وَّبَارِكْ وَسَلِّمْ ـ [8]

---

[5] O Servants of Allah! I remind you of the coming of His days and admonish you to adopt righteousness of heart. *Verily, he who comes to his Lord a sinner— for him is hell; he shall neither die therein nor live.* (*Surah Taa haa,* 20:75) [Publisher]

[6] Do not be ensnared by the beauty and adornment of this world. *And seek help with patience and Prayer;* (*Surah Al-Baqarah,* 2:46) [Publisher]

[7] *Allah and His angels send blessings on the Prophet. O ye who believe! You also should invoke blessings on him and salute him with the salutation of peace.* (*Surah Al-Ahzaab,* 33:57) [Publisher]

[8] We invoke your grace and blessings on Muhammad and his Ummah. [Publisher]

Prophecy about the Plague in Verse

نشان اگرچہ نہ در اختیار کس بود ست

مگر نشان بدہم از نشان زِ دا دارم

کہ آن سعید زِ طاعون نجات خواہد یافت

کہ جَست و جُست پناہے بچار دیوارم

مرا قسم بخداوند خویش و عظمتِ او

کہ ہست ایں ہمہ از وحی پاک گفتارم

چہ حاجت است بہ بحثِ دِگر ہمیں کافیست

برائے آنکہ سیہ شد دلش زِ انکارم

اگر دروغ برآید ہر آنچہ وعدۂ من

رواست گر ہمہ خیزند بہر پیکارم۔ [9]

---

[9] Although it is not within the power of anyone to show a sign,
  But I show you a sign from God.
Such a fortunate one shall be delivered from the plague,
  Who fears [God] and seeks refuge in the four walls of my home.
I swear by God and by His Majesty,
  All my words flow from divine revelation.
So what is there to quarrel with now, this should suffice,
  For anyone whose heart has fallen dark due to rejecting me.
If the promise that I have made proves false,
  It is only right that everyone stands up to fight against me.
[Publisher]

A Request for Donations

For an Extension of 'the House'

In anticipation of the likely dissemination of the plague throughout the country, it has been noted that there is a dire shortage of space in my home, part of which is occupied by male guests and another part by female guests. As you are aware, Allah Exalted be His Glory has promised to especially safeguard all those who dwell within its four walls. My partners in the inheritance of the late Ghulam Haider's home have agreed to give over to me my stake and sell to me its remaining portion as well. In my view this house, which can become an extension to my home, can be prepared within a cost of two thousand. Since there is a danger that the time of this plague is near and in accordance with the glad-tiding of divine revelation this home will serve as an ark in the storm of this plague, no one knows how many persons might benefit from the promise of this glad-tiding, therefore, this work is of immediate nature. We ought to trust in God who is the Creator, the Provider and the One who sees our good deeds and make every effort in His cause. Although this home of mine is like an ark, it can no longer accommodate any further men or women—therefore an extension is necessary.

والسّلام على من اتبع الهدٰى [*Peace be on those who follow guidance*].

Announced by,

Mirza Ghulam Ahmad of Qadian

Glossary

Aameen – A term which literally means 'so let it be' and is used at the end of a supplication to pray that God may accept it. It is similar in meaning to 'amen.'

Ahl-e-Hadith – Literally means, 'The People of Hadith.' This is a sect of Islam which believes that the Hadith of the Holy Prophet[sa] take precedence over the Holy Quran as a primary source for theology. In general it may also refer to those who give preference to oral tradition over divine scripture.

Bai'at – Oath of allegiance to a religious leader; initiation at the hands of a Prophet or his Khalifah. Literally means 'to be sold'.

Hadith – Sayings of the Holy Prophet Muhammad[sa].

Hajj – Pilgrimage to the Ka'bah, which takes place once a year. All Muslims who are able must perform the pilgrimage at least once in their lifetime as a pillar of faith.

Imam Mahdi – A title meaning 'Guided Leader,' given to the Reformer of the Latter Days prophesied by the Holy Prophet Muhammad[sa].

Insha'Allah – Literally means, 'If Allah wills' and is a phrase used by Muslims as a prayer to seek blessings from Allah to accomplish any task.

Jizyah – A tax paid in lieu of military service by non-Muslims living in a Muslim State in return for which non-Muslim citizens were guaranteed protection from external and internal aggression.

Khalifah – Caliph is derived from the Arabic word *Khalifah*, which means 'successor'. In Islamic terminology, the word righteous *Khalifah* is applied to one of the four *Khulafa* who continued the mission of the Holy Prophet Muhammad^{sa}, the Holy Prophet of Islam. Ahmadi Muslims refer to a successor of the Promised Messiah^{as} as Khalifatul-Masih. *Khulafa* is the plural of *Khalifah*.

Khaatam-ul-Anbiyaa – The Seal of the Prophets, a title accorded to the Holy Prophet Muhammad^{sa}.

Khaatam-ul-Khulafaa – Literally means the Seal of the Caliphs.

Khatm-e-Nubuwwat – Refers to the lofty status granted to the Holy Prophet^{sa} and means 'Seal of Prophethood'. In other words, it infers that all the qualities and attributes of prophethood have reached their final point of perfection in the person of the Prophet Muhammad^{sa}.

Khula – The legal right endowed to a woman in the Islamic Shariah to seek a divorce.

Mahram – Mahram is a term in Islamic jurisprudence which refers to such men or women with whom marriage is impermissible.

Mi'raaj – A spiritual experience of the Prophet Muhammad where he ascended into the heavens.

Nabi – Literally means 'Prophet' and is a term used in the Holy Quran to refer to someone who receives abundant news of the unseen from God.

Qawwali – A style of music employed by certain Sufi sects within Islam as a form of devotion and worship.

Rak'at – One cycle in the formal prayer observed by Muslims, which consists of standing and bowing positions as well as prostration.

Sunnah – Practice of the Holy Prophet^{sa}.

Surah – A chapter of the Holy Quran

Zakat – The fourth pillar in Islam known as obligatory almsgiving, which constitutes the social support system in Islam for the distribution of wealth. The poor and needy are provided for by the contributions of the rich and affluent. Literally means, 'increase' or 'purification.'

Index

S

T

V